# Green Design

Design for the Environment

Published 1991 by Laurence King Ltd

British Library Cataloguing in Publication Data
Mackenzie, Dorothy
    Green design: design for the environment
    1.    Design. Conservation
    I.    Title
    333.72

ISBN 1-85669-001-6

Designed by Wade Greenwood
Printed and bound in China
Printed on minimum-chlorine-bleached paper

**Acknowledgements**
Many people have made this book possible. I would like to
thank, in particular, Louise Moss and Julia Engelhardt, whose
persistent research helped track down so many of the examples
featured in this book, all the companies and individuals who
provided information and photographs, and my editor, Jane
Havell, who proposed the book in the first place, and whose
encouragement and deadlines ensured that it came to fruition.
I would also like to acknowledge the influence of John Elkington
in the thinking behind the book. His booklet, *The Green Designer*,
published in 1986, set out important guidelines and directions,
which I hope this book amplifies. Many other friends and
colleagues contributed to the development of ideas, and my
husband Stephen provided support and help throughout.
*Dorothy Mackenzie*

# Green Design

## Design for the Environment

Dorothy Mackenzie

Researchers

Louise Moss

Julia Engelhardt

Laurence King

# Contents

# Foreword

◄ A wind farm near Palm Springs, California (see page 24).

The purpose of this book is to raise awareness among all those involved in the design process of the relationship between design decisions and environment issues, and to demonstrate the significance of the designer's contribution to minimising environmental problems. It is intended primarily to help designers ask the right questions, rather than to deliver unequivocal answers. We are still at the very earliest stage of understanding. Many issues are not yet fully understood, contradictions abound, new solutions are emerging all the time. Despite this confusion, however, some guidelines are emerging, and many people are experimenting with new design ideas.

Some background to major environmental issues is covered, although the book focuses on the implications of the issues for the design process. A wide range of excellent detailed reference books are available, some of which are listed at the end. Examples are used throughout to demonstrate work that has already begun; none of the examples represents the unachievable "green product", and there will inevitably by many aspects of some examples which could be criticised. In some cases, the motivation behind the work may have been cost or aesthetic considerations rather than environment consciousness. However, each illustrates an interesting direction or a partial solution, and may stimulate other ideas.

Examples are drawn from the work of major multinational companies and individual designer-makers, from well-known consultancies and from students. The largest companies often have the technical know-how and resources needed to address major problems and to develop innovative solutions, while many very interesting and fundamental approaches are being examined by individual designers. While the vast majority of examples are in commercial production, a few are still in concept form. Designs from Third World countries usually receive insufficient attention; there is much to learn from areas where resource conservation and energy efficiency are already practical necessities.

One objective of this book is to demonstrate that designs which take account of environment considerations can be commercially successful, functional and highly aesthetically attractive. There is little point in producing environmentally sensitive solutions if they are too expensive, inconvenient or unattractive for anyone to want to buy and use them. There is no reason why designing for minimal environment impact should produce drab, poor-quality results which give satisfaction only through guilt reduction.

The incredible rate of change in the solutions available and in the development of new thinking means that any book on this subject is always out of date. For that reason, detailed technical information on materials and production techniques has been avoided; it is always best to check directly with manufacturers or professional associations for the latest developments.

The need to build consideration of environment impact into the design process will pose enormous problems and challenges, but it will also be a stimulus for innovation and creativity. Above all, it will provide real opportunities for designers to demonstrate the value of their problem-solving skills and the breadth of their contribution.

# 1    Introduction

"In this age of mass production when everything must be planned and designed, design has become the most powerful tool with which man shapes his tools and environments (and, by extension, society and himself). This demands high social and moral responsibility from the designer." (Victor Papanek, *Design for the Real World*, 1970)

The idea that designers should take into consideration the environment impact of their work is not new. Twenty years ago Victor Papanek argued convincingly that the designer was in a powerful position, able to help create a better world, or contribute further to planetary destruction. His ideas - that designers should resist designing built-in obsolescence; that consumers' needs, rather than their wants, should be addressed; and that designers should strive to find ways of using their skills for socially useful ends, especially in developing countries - outraged much of the design establishment at the time.

Today, however, ideas which once seemed utopian and naive appear highly relevant and almost inevitable, given the unprecedented levels of concern being expressed throughout the world over environmental problems. Twenty years ago, environmentalism was regarded as an activity for the radical fringe; now, governments strive to demonstrate their environmentalist credentials, and problems attract high levels of popular concern. There is a growing consensus that problems affecting the environment cannot be ignored. As a result of dramatic scientific evidence of ozone depletion and new scientific agreement about the impending problems of global warming, a new sense of urgency has arisen.

Rising public concern is being translated into action in many countries: people are demonstrating their feelings through their voting preferences, by joining environment campaigning groups, by changing their behaviour to accommodate recycling or energy efficiency, and by using environment criteria in their purchasing decisions as consumers.

We are entering a period when environment performance, together with a wide range of ethical and moral issues, will be on the agenda for business, government and individuals. New criteria will evolve for judging the acceptability of products and processes; new methods will emerge to calculate the true cost of activities; new regulations will control industrial and individual behaviour. Decisions about the nature of our society and economy may well be underpinned by a growing commitment to sustainable rather than uncontrolled development.

Are designers equipped to respond to the new demands which will arise from these changes? The answer is almost certainly no, as it must be for almost all professionals trained without reference to the environment impact of their activities.

In most places, design has not been taught in the context of its social and ecological impact. Many designers assume that their area of responsibility is limited to function and appearance. In some fields, most notably architecture, a broader view has sometimes been taken because of the scale of the direct impact of buildings on their local environment. But even here, little attention has been paid to the implications of the type of construction materials used or, for example, to the energy efficiency of the lighting system.

One might be able to argue that up until now designing with environment impact in mind was a matter of personal taste or individual moral responsibility. Now it is clear that it will become a commercial imperative. The value and role of designers will be substantially reduced if they cannot incorporate new concepts and new criteria into their work.

▼ Exterior of the corporate headquarters of the NMB Bank in The Netherlands, designed by Alberts and Van Huut for energy efficiency and employee satisfaction. The natural environment has proved hugely popular with the staff working there (for a detailed analysis, see pages 56-9).

| The growth in membership of leading US environmental organisations, 1970 - 1990 | | | | | |
|---|---|---|---|---|---|
| | 1970 | 1975 | 1980 | 1985 | 1990 |
| National Wildlife Federation | 2.6m | n/a | 4.6m | 4.5m | 5.8m |
| Sierra Club | 114,000 | 153,000 | 182,000 | 363,000 | 566,000 |
| National Audubon Society | 105,000 | 255,000 | 310,000 | 425,000 | 515,000 |
| Wilderness Society | 66,000 | n/a | 63,000 | 97,000 | 363,000 |
| Environmental Defence Fund | 10,000 | 40,000 | 45,000 | 50,000 | 150,000 |
| Greenpeace | * | 6,000 | 80,000 | 450,000 | 2.0m |
| Natural Resources Defence Council | ** | 15,000 | 35,000 | 65,000 | 140,000 |

* founded 1971      ** founded 1970      source: *The Economist*

◄ ➤ A semi-buried house designed by Javier Barba in Catalunya, Spain. The soil provides natural insulation and maintains stable internal temperatures throughout the year, minimising any need for extra heating. South-facing windows and glazed doors maximise solar gain, while the tiled floors store heat. Shutters and a canvas awning help regulate the heat during the summer. The roof is covered with grass to help integrate the house into its surroundings (compare the house in Denmark shown on page 47). With the glazed south face providing light and panoramic views, there is little sense of living underground. This house was featured as a case study by Project Monitor, an EC initiative to study passive solar architecture.

There is an opportunity for designers to show imagination and leadership, pioneering the way forward and solving real problems.

For many years, designers have been asserting their influence and demonstrating the power of design. The new demands of designing for minimum ecological impact will provide an ideal platform from which designers can justify their claims and acknowledge their responsibilities.

## The role and responsibility of the designer

Why should so much responsibility fall to the designer? Design is one part of a holistic process, which involves a wide range of other skills. However, design is a pivotal part of the process.

Many environmental problems are caused by the pollution which results from the production and use of products and services, particularly mass-produced

---

**Sustainable development**

Sustainable development was defined by the Bruntland Commission (The World Commission on Environment and Development, published in 1987) as meeting "the needs of the present without compromising the ability of future generations to meet their own needs." The implication is that for development to be sustainable, it must take account not just of economic factors, but also of environmental and social factors, and must assess long-term consequences of actions as well as short-term results.

For industry, the implications of sustainable development include taking a much longer-term view of investment decisions and taking all the true, external costs of activities into account. Such approaches are made difficult by the short-term focus of financial and shareholder interests in many Western countries.

The concept of sustainable development, or "green growth", exists in most countries only as a philosophical ideal. However, the Dutch National Environment Plan acknowledges sustainable economic development as its guiding principle.

products. Most products and services use up natural resources, many of which are irreplaceable. The method by which raw materials are extracted from the earth can cause severe local environmental problems. The manufacturing process itself uses energy, creates waste, and may result in harmful by-products. The product has then to be distributed - raising other environmental issues - following which it is used. Many products have a significant effect on the environment when in use - cars, for example, or detergents, or paints. And finally, the product may be disposed of, causing another set of problems.

The designer, as the principal determinant or creator of the product itself, has a direct influence on the amount of damage which will occur at each stage in the process. What materials will be used, and from where will these be obtained? How will the product be manufactured? Are particular processes required to give a specific effect or appearance? How will the product be used and disposed of - is it designed to be easy to repair, or to be thrown away? If it is to be disposed of, can parts of it be reused or recycled? Designers, as creators or specifiers, are in a position to determine many of these issues.

But designers also influence environment impact indirectly, through their role as setters of styles and tastes. Might the focus of design attention be on the development of faddish trivia, the constant search for novelty, for the sake of novelty? In some countries, most notably the UK, the Eighties saw a dramatic rise in the recognition of the importance of good design. But by the end of the decade the word "designer" had become devalued almost to the point of becoming pejorative, because it had become associated with superficial glitziness, with a proliferation of expensive, unnecessary objects whose sole purpose was to convey social status upon their owners. Design was criticised as elitist, and was seen to be relevant to only a narrow area of activities - primarily industries making consumer goods. Designers have participated fully in the disposable society, creating new styles with increasing frequency, and therefore necessarily building in obsolescence. They have often been criticised by environmentalists for failing to use their skills and influence to useful purpose.

Until now, many designers may have felt that, if they wished to use their skills, they have had no alternative but to participate in the misuse of design. Now, however, as individual values and business priorities are beginning to change, they have the opportunity to demonstrate that environmental considerations, along with social and ethical concerns, occupy a central position within mainstream design thinking.

Designers can now speak from an authoritative platform in most countries, and they increasingly occupy key positions in major companies. The contribution that design can make to business performance is now widely recognised, and many governments have been active in encouraging industry to work closely with designers to improve the quality and competitiveness of their products and services.

> "There are many ingredients for success in the market place. But I am convinced that British industry will never compete if it forgets the importance of good design. By 'design' I do not just mean appearance. I mean all the engineering and industrial design that goes into a product from the idea stage to the production stage, and which is so important in ensuring that it works, that it is reliable, that it is good value and that it looks good. In short, it is good design which makes people buy products and which gives products a good name. It is essential to the future of our industry."
> (Margaret Thatcher, UK Prime Minister, 1982)

The role of designers as the link between the manufacturing process and the customer, between technical and marketing requirements, has given them a central position in many companies in areas such as new product development. This position must now be justified: designers must demonstrate an ability to take on the complex and challenging issues which surround designing for minimum environment impact. This will require a willingness to undertake thorough research before starting the design process, and an understanding of environment issues and the ability to know where to look for guidance. Some technical understanding of the production process and of the properties of materials will also be essential for the environment-conscious designer.

## The commercial imperative

Many businesses are beginning to realise that long-term commercial success depends on acceptable environment performance. Environmental problems such as resource depletion and pollution are disruptive and costly, and poor environment performance, such as industrial accidents, can call into question the social acceptability of a company. The suspicion which many people feel about "big business" is legitimised by any evidence of a careless approach to the protection of the environment.

Poor environment performance can also considerably reduce the attractiveness of a company for investment purposes. The emergence of green and ethical investment funds has given companies an added incentive to prove that they follow high standards of environment performance. The introduction of the Valdez Principles in the USA, following the disaster of the oil spillage from the Exxon Valdez tanker in Alaska in 1989, has created a substantial sum of investment funds which will flow only to those companies who have signed the demanding guidelines (see opposite).

Many of the large companies regarded as being the leaders in their fields are now incorporating environment criteria into their definition of "quality", through programmes such as Total Quality Management. Some have practised several aspects of good environment performance for many years, inspired by a desire to reduce waste. 3M's "Pollution Prevention Pays" programme (see page 15), and Dow Chemical's "Waste Reduction Always Pays", are good examples of companies identifying a commercial benefit in sound environmental practices.

Many of the most active programmes have been in industries at the forefront of environmental problems, such as the chemicals industry and the oil industry, but such programmes are now beginning to gain acceptance across a much wider spectrum. Up until now, however, the majority of companies which have considered environment issues at all have done so because they were forced by legislation to address problems they themselves were causing - such as river pollution or the emission of harmful gases - or because there were substantial cost savings to be achieved, or because of issues related to the health and safety of their workforce. Now there are a number of additional pressures, which will mean that environment issues will move increasingly centre-stage for industry.

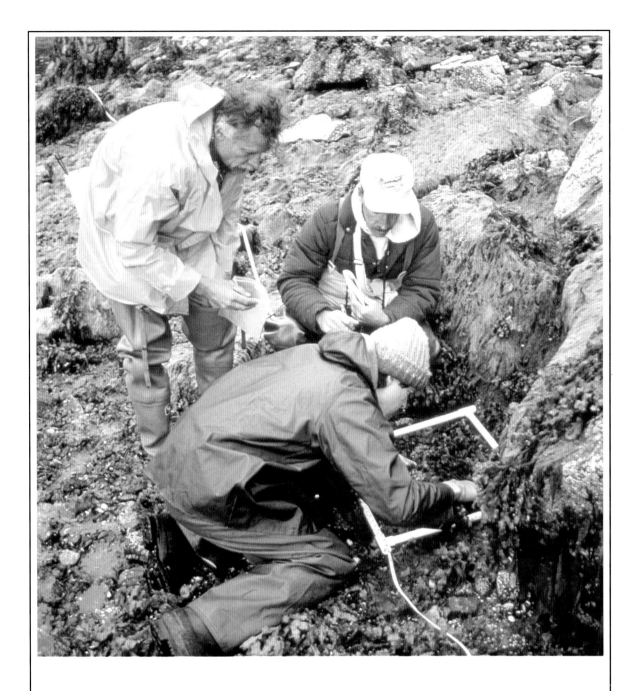

▲ Biologists
examine the shore
after the giant
supertanker Exxon
Valdez went aground
in March 1989 in
Prince William Sound
in Alaska. More than
10 million gallons of
oil escaped, polluting
over 700 miles of
coastline and killing
millions of fish, birds
and other wildlife.

### The Valdez Principles

The code of practical guidelines for corporate
behaviour was published in September 1989 by
the Coalition for Environmentally Responsible
Economies, a group composed of
environmentalists and ethical investment
organisations. The principles are intended to
help industry develop its own policies and
practices, and to guide investors on their
decisions by identifying which companies
subscribe to the principles. They are:

● Protection of the biosphere

● Sustainable use of natural resources

● Reduction and disposal of waste

● Wise use of energy

● Risk reduction

● Marketing of safe products and
services

● Damage compensation

● Disclosure of information

● Appointing an environment director and
managers

● Undertaking environmental assessments
and annual audits

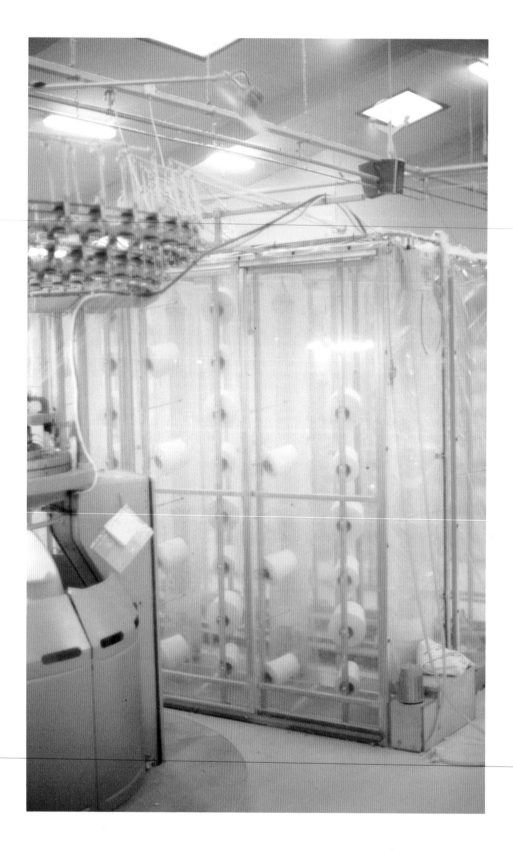

▲ Part of the factory
producing Novotex
"green cotton" in
Denmark (see pages
146-7). The glassed-in
sections protect
workers from the
health hazards
associated with cotton
particles in the air.

## 3M

The US-based multinational company 3M has pursued a policy of trying to reduce pollution at source wherever possible, rather than relying on controlling it once it has been created. The "Pollution Prevention Pays" programme encourages individuals or groups of employees to identify ways of preventing pollution through modifying processes, developing improved products, re-designing equipment and finding new uses for waste. The programme has resulted in major cost savings for the company, as well as the avoidance of large quantities of pollution.

## New legislative frameworks

Increasing public concern has led to demands for more and more legislation to control industrial activity. The extent of legislation varies considerably between countries, and even within parts of a country, but there is universal belief that the amount of legislation will increase. Already in some countries laws determine what materials a soft drinks container may be made of.

A number of clear themes are emerging from legislation being introduced all over Europe, North America and Australia:

● The polluter pays.

● The producer should bear responsibility for waste disposal.

● The public should have access to information on companies' environment performance.

Meeting new legislative demands such as these will require significant changes in some industries, and will change priorities especially in areas such as product design. A manufacturer charged with the responsibility of taking back used cars for final disposal will have an incentive to ensure that cars are designed in the first place for easy disassembly for recycling, or that no harmful emissions are given off if final residues have to be incinerated.

## Employee pressure

Many developed countries are facing the prospect of a decline in the number of people making up the skilled workforce. Competition for the best employees will grow tougher, and companies will have to make themselves as attractive as possible to secure the right people. There is now a very high level of concern over environmental issues amongst younger people, particularly those in higher education, which means that, increasingly, companies' environment performance will be assessed by any potential recruits as a key issue when they are considering employment. Already, company recruitment literature is emphasising environment commitment in recognition that this may be a crucial deciding factor.

Maintaining the loyalty and commitment of the workforce will also demand that the goals and values of the company are compatible with the goals and values of individuals; as the latter are changing to place a higher importance on environment protection, so company values will have to change too, to avoid the alienation of employees. And, of course, many people working within companies who see themselves as determined environmentalists will gradually appear in senior management positions. The marketing director of one major multinational company, when asked which environmental campaigning group gave him the toughest time and presented him with the most challenges, replied that his toughest critics came from inside the company, from the junior members of his own department.

## The Dutch National Environment Plan

The National Environment Plan is a far-reaching, comprehensive, 200-point plan which aims to re-orient the Dutch economy over the next twenty years. It calls for dramatic reductions in pollution, setting specific targets by the year 2000, such as:

● 55 per cent of the total waste stream should be re-used, and 10 per cent prevented.

● There should be a 50 per cent reduction in the use of pesticides.

● 25 per cent extra energy conservation should be achieved in space heating in buildings.

The plan states that public transport will be preferred to private cars; that manufacturers may be required to take back used products, and that producers may be liable to pay the cost of environmental damage caused by their products.

➤ One of the largest supermarkets in Denmark, Irma banned the use of PVC in May 1990, forcing suppliers to use other packaging materials. The company established its own technical research programme to evaluate and develop alternatives. This move is part of an overall "going green" policy, which includes stocking a wide range of environmentally responsible products.

# Personlig pleje uden PVC.
# Det virker både i
# dybden og i længden.

Irma har udviklet en ny hudplejeserie, der først og fremmest går i hudens dybde og virker efter de metoder, der i dag kendes som de bedste. Det er lette, milde cremer, og De kan vælge, om De vil pleje Dem selv med eller uden parfume.

Når den nye hudplejeserie også virker i længden, skyldes det den miljørigtige emballage. For nok er alt det, man har stående på badeværelseshylden en personlig sag. Men det er forurening af vore omgivelser til gengæld ikke. Hidtil er de fleste plastemballager

til hudplejemidler blevet fremstillet med PVC. Et stof, der blandt andet udvikler klor ved forbrænding.

Denne forurening vil Irma gerne være med til at sætte en stopper for. Derfor er emballagen til den nye hudplejeserie uden PVC. I stedet har vi brugt en miljørigtig plast, der ikke skader, men indgår i naturens kredsløb ved forbrænding sammen med det øvrige husholdningsaffald. Det fremgår også af det lille "indgår i naturens kredsløb" mærke, som er præget i bunden. Og som i øvrigt sid-

der på flere og flere af vore emballager. I 1990 tager vi skridtet fuldt ud, og forbyder alle former for PVC-emballager i vore butikker. Den tid, den glæde.

Velkommen i Irma.

Til alle, der tænker, før de handler.

## Market demand

In addition to financial, legislative and employee pressure, market pressure is playing a major role in encouraging changes in industrial behaviour. Some large organisations have introduced "Suppliers' Charters", setting out the environment performance they require from anyone supplying them with a product or service. Government departments and institutions in Germany, for example, are required to purchase products such as recycled paper; major retailers such as Wal-Mart in the US and Tesco in the UK are advising their suppliers on the development of lower-impact products, and on aspects of good environment practice such as energy efficiency. Retailers in several countries have been quick to respond to consumer pressure, and have often initiated their own specific campaigns. The commercial risk of failing to anticipate environmental problems can be considerable. Entire markets can now disappear almost overnight, as was the case with the market for CFC gases in aerosols. So it is very much in the interests of indus-

try to follow the environment debate closely, and try to keep ahead of legislation at all times.

Environment pressures do not just create problems and commercial risks, however; they also bring about major new market opportunities. Obvious examples are in the rapidly growing field of pollution-abatement technology, but improved environment performance provides an attractive new benefit in many sectors, and has led to significant competitive advantage for many companies.

## What about the cost?

A frequent complaint about improving environment performance, and one of the main reasons given for failing to adopt high standards, is the assumption that higher costs are always involved. In many areas additional cost is inevitable if, for example, the price of making good the damage done to water courses, seas or the atmosphere through the emission of waste materials has not previously been considered. The cost of safely disposing of products at the end of their life can also be high.

Concerns are expressed about passing this higher cost on to the customer, particularly in markets facing competition from companies or countries which do not adopt higher environmental standards and can therefore keep prices lower.

On the other hand, the savings that can be made from minimising waste, increasing energy efficiency and not over-specifying the quality of materials needed are frequently under-estimated. Of course, customers would prefer to have good-quality products, offering good environmental performance, at no extra cost: this is the new challenge for designers. Can products be re-thought so that they deliver the same benefit to the user, in a way that is environmentally better, but at no extra cost? In some sectors, the customer may be required to pay a higher price for the product, but the trade-off may be a longer-lived, more reliable product, or one that consumes less energy in use, thus leading to savings in the longer term.

Some companies have of course viewed the development of consumer interest in the environment as a short-term

◄ This take-away packaging for the US restaurant Toulouse by Duffy Design is made from brown recycled card. The design aims to communicate the casual, fun element of fast food.

➤ Low-energy halogen bulbs were used in the lighting system designed for the St Anne's Shopping Centre in Harrow, England, by David Davies Associates and lighting consultant Shiv Kaykan.

marketing opportunity. Taking advantage of consumers' lack of knowledge, they have used minor improvements as the basis for dramatic "green product" claims, often identified by large green labels, proclaiming the product to be "environment friendly". Sometimes the apparent greenness of the product has camouflaged a poor environment performance in other aspects of the company's activities - in the supply chain, or in the manufacturing process itself. Companies perceived by consumers to be jumping on the bandwagon in this way are likely to be strongly criticised, and will therefore not be successful in the long term unless they can substantiate their claims with a satisfactory all-round performance.

The introduction of official "green product" labelling schemes may serve to bring a common point of reference into increasingly confusing consumer markets, where claims and counter-claims about the performance of different products can undermine consumer confidence and lead to cynicism.

Pressures from the market place, from legislation, from investors and shareholders, and from their own employees, are going to ensure that businesses cannot ignore environmental issues; rather, they will adopt them as a central aspect of business strategy. Good environment performance will increasingly be seen as a prerequisite of good management practice. Suppliers of public services and government departments will find that they are expected to give full regard to environment issues, due to pressures from public opinion, employees and their governments.

So, for the designer, the ability to understand the environment impact of design decisions will no longer be an

◄ Compact fluorescent lightbulbs can last up to eight times longer than incandescent light bulbs and use about 80 per cent less energy to produce the same brightness. Replacing a 75-watt incandescent bulb with an 18-watt compact fluorescent bulb will, over the lifetime of the bulb, avoid emitting the equivalent of 1,000 lb of carbon dioxide and about 20 lb of sulphur dioxide from a typical power-generating plant in the USA.

**Green labelling schemes**

The growth of consumer interest in the environment performance of products has led some countries to introduce official "Eco-labelling" schemes, to help consumers make an informed choice. The German Blue Angel scheme (label, right), established in 1978, covers over 3,000 products. Canada's Environment Choice scheme, established in 1989, uses a cradle-to-grave assessment system, as does the Japanese eco-mark. A Europe-wide scheme is being developed, with a multi-criteria basis for assessment. One result of the introduction of official labelling schemes is that manufacturers and designers are given some guidelines within which to work; there is also less danger of consumer confusion about the legitimacy of a claim.

▼ Advertisement for "eco-beer" from the Lammbrau brewery in Neumarkt, Germany, which aims for a comprehensive approach to environment performance. The beer itself is made from organically grown ingredients, with no additives. The plant has a heat recycling installation, and solar energy is used to dry some of the ingredients. The product is distributed only in bottles, which are re-usable, and the labels contain only paper, without the metallic foil customarily wrapped round the neck.

optional extra, but rather an essential part of design skills. "Green design" should not be seen as a sub-set of "mainstream design", but as an essential and integral component of the design process - as important as producability, function and aesthetics.

## The rise of the green consumer

The willingness of consumers in many countries to regard environmental benefit as a purchasing criterion has resulted in the emergence of new products, new selling platforms and new advertising themes. In markets as diverse as household cleaners and holidays, office stationery and tee-shirts, investment funds and buildings, green advantages are highlighted in the hope that this will attract purchasers. A rash of books and magazines has appeared, advising readers on how to be a green consumer, and providing extensive and varied guidance on what to buy and what to do.

What has happened to make individual consumers so interested in environment performance?

People have been concerned about environmental problems for many years, but levels of interest began to climb in many countries in the mid-Eighties, when increasing evidence emerged of the problems. The destruction of German forests and Scandinavian lakes by acid rain; the overflowing, contaminating landfill sites on the North East coast of the USA; choking smog in Milan; the elimination of entire species through the destruction of local habitats - all of these were tangible evidence of the harm being done to ecology and to people. The emergence of a scientific consensus about major problems such as ozone depletion and the greenhouse effect encouraged many people to accept that warnings about the consequences of environmental neglect could not be dismissed as the ravings of doom-proclaiming extremists.

Concern about environmental issues is not simply altruistic; fears about personal health and safety, and about the safety and future of children, inspire many activities. The realisation that the ozone hole could increase the risk of skin cancer was probably the most significant contributor to

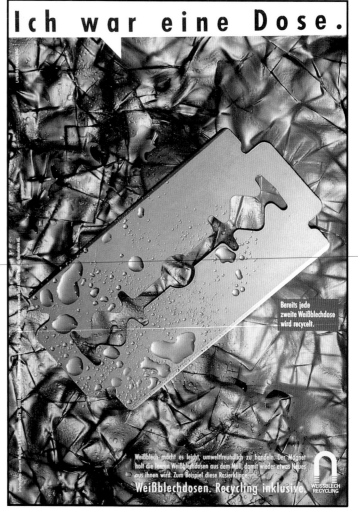

public willingness to switch from CFCs in aerosols in the UK.

Growing affluence in the developed world has afforded many people the luxury of being able to be interested in the quality of their lives, rather than simply in survival through the acquisition of basic necessities. But material well-being does not lead automatically to a high quality of life. There is little point in owning a smart car if it is impossible to drive it anywhere because of road congestion. Environmental and quality of life benefits become "added value" benefits, for which affluent people are prepared to pay, particularly if these allow them to enjoy their material wealth in safety and peace of mind.

Individuals who feel concerned about environmental issues tend to want to try to "do their bit" to help address the problems - or at least to try not to contribute to even greater problems. Only a tiny minority believe that the government and industry alone should do everything; most want to feel involved, and eagerly seek out information which will advise them on how they can help. One of the simplest and least painful ways of feeling involved

**◄ ►** These advertisements, put out by the German Tin Information Centre, show products made from recycled tin. The headline reads "I was a can": in Germany every second tin can is recyled. Much of the recycled metal is used for high-quality products for which manufacturers have traditionally chosen virgin material, but they certainly do not suffer either in quality or aesthetic appearance.

**▲** Guidebooks such as these give advice on issues from pollution to energy efficiency, Third World trade to animal welfare, identifying which products and brands represent the best, and worst, environmental options.

➤ **The GE Generation 2 Battery Charger for New York-based consultancy Cousins Design recharges up to eight batteries in only one hour, and then reduces the current until it is ready for use again, using the minimum amount of energy. Rechargeable batteries help to reduce the problems caused by battery disposal, but the recharge time has traditionally been long and energy consumption high.**

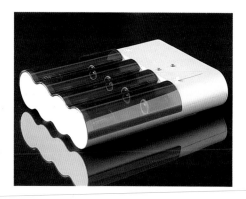

is by buying "green products". With often a small effort, people can make a contribution to minimising damage. Environmentalists have of course been quick to point out, quite correctly, that it is dangerous to mislead people into thinking that buying a different brand of washing powder will save the world. Radical changes in behaviour and reductions in consumption will be essential. But green consumerism can be a starting-point for more fundamental changes, if it goes hand in hand with a genuine education process. Consumption will always continue, and it is therefore legitimate to attempt to make its impact as minimal as possible.

The translation of hitherto vague expressions of concern into practical demonstrations of purchasing power is having a significant impact on business, and has also helped to keep up pressure on politicians.

### Does green consumerism work?

*Changes to existing products*
Many products have already been modified to incorporate better environment

performance. Recycled paper in household products, recycled plastic in garbage sacks and elimination of phosphates from detergents have all been presented as straightforward product improvements, designed to add an attractive competitive benefit to the product.

*Opportunities for small companies*
A few small companies have been selling environmentally conscious products for many years. Many of these have recently experienced dramatic increases in demand, and an acceptance into mainstream distribution channels. Often the small size of the companies has meant that the products have to sell at a significant premium over major brands, but this has not prevented major increases in sales.

*Penetration of new geographic markets*
With Germany consistently in the forefront of concern and action over environmental issues, in many sectors German products are more environment-conscious than those from other countries. Varta, Europe's largest battery manufacturer, has now secured a strong position in the UK market, with its mercury-free and cadmium-free batteries: within twelve months its market share was boosted from 2 per cent to 17 per cent - a major challenge to its competitors, Duracell and Ever Ready.

*Retailers take the initiative*
Several major retailers have used the rise of the green consumer to strengthen their own image and consolidate their relationships with customers through the provision of information and a wide range of own-label products, selected for their green credentials.

➤ **Varta, Europe's largest battery manufacturer, produce mercury- and cadmium-free batteries as part of their minimum environment impact initiative. They have changed packaging from blister packs to cartons made entirely from recycled board.**

### Who are the green consumers?

Survey evidence shows that concern about environment issues, and expressions of willingness to take action, are widespread across all income groups and regions but higher among the better-educated and more affluent consumers. Women consistently show the highest levels of concern and desire to participate, which has important implications on products designed with a female target market in mind. Young people are also likely to be particularly environment-conscious, and this has major implications for markets in the future. The issues that people are most concerned about vary from country to country, but broadly reflect the focus of media campaigns and perceived major threats.

### What do people expect of green products?

Some of the earliest products which offered environment benefits were significantly different from their conventional counterparts in terms of their performance. For many consumers, a reduction in functional performance was hard to accept, especially when combined with a higher price. While, over time, expectations can be modified, particularly when these relate mainly to appearance, during the initial stages the more successful products have been those which perform very similarly to conventional products. For example, the removal of bleaches and optical brightening agents from detergents produced a laundry result that some found unacceptable. Changes in car performance caused by lead-free petrol also proved unpopular with sports car enthusiasts. The move away from chlorine bleaching of babies' disposable diapers, however, resulted in a change of colour from brilliant white to cream which customers found acceptable, since appearance only was involved.

The production of less environmentally harmful products which can compete directly on performance with traditional products is a major challenge. In some sectors it may simply not be possible, and consumer expectations may eventually modify. The answer may lie in a radical new solution which challenges the conventional approach by asking, "Why does the product have to be like this?" It is in this direction that the real opportunity for worthwhile innovation lies.

### Loblaws

In 1989 Loblaws, the Canadian supermarket chain, introduced a range of over a hundred products under the "Green Line" label. They met with considerable success, but the environmental campaigning group Pollution Probe was criticised by some for endorsing them, on the grounds that they were not all as green as they should be.

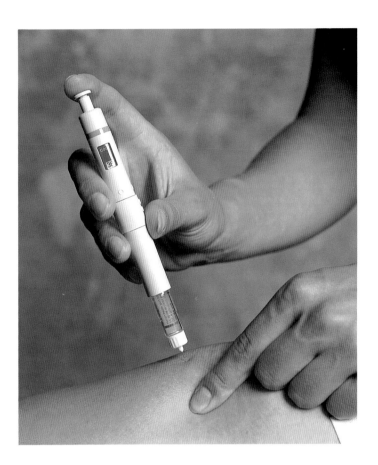

▲ Novopen 11 is a convenient and discreet insulin injection system designed to make diabetes easier to live with. Designed by Sams Design in London for Danish insulin producer Novo, the pen offers safety, accuracy and simplicity. The design has won several awards for its imaginative user-friendliness.

# 2     The background to environment issues

Of the many important environment problems we confront, this chapter details the issues of which designers should be especially aware. The role of designers in addressing these issues goes far beyond the contribution that the actions of any individual citizen or consumer can make.

➤ A wind farm near Palm Springs, California. Wind turbines are being used in some countries to generate electricity; large areas of land are required, although they could be built off shore. Wind power represents a relatively cheap, clean and simple form of alternative power, if enough can be generated.

It is sometimes difficult to see how individual decisions by designers, about what appear to be rather minor issues - such as the selection of one material over another - affect global environment problems. But design can have an impact upon the environment in many different ways: through the extraction of raw materials; through the design of the manufacturing process; in how the product is used and distributed, and in what happens when the product reaches the end of its useful life.

## The greenhouse effect, or global warming

Gases in the atmosphere insulate the earth, preventing some of the sun's heat, reflected from the earth's surface, from escaping into space. This is a natural effect without which the world would be frozen. But industrialisation and agricultural development have resulted in increases in the concentration of some gases in the atmosphere, trapping more heat. The main cause is an increase of 25 per cent in the last two hundred years in the amount of carbon dioxide produced by the burning of wood, oil and coal. Other gases, such as methane, chlorofluorocarbons (CFCs) and nitrous oxide are also playing a role. The effect of increasing concentrations of greenhouse gases could be to cause a significant increase in the global annual mean temperature: estimates vary, but even a 1 degree rise would have serious implications in terms of regional climatic changes, rises in sea levels and redistribution of areas of land suitable for agricultural production. World energy use doubled between 1930 and 1960, and doubled again between 1960 and 1984, the vast majority of the energy supply coming from oil, coal and gas.

Discussions of ways to avert global warming have focused on the need to reduce emissions of carbon dioxide, for example by extracting it from power stations; on the importance of developing alternatives to fossil fuels; on the need to preserve the earth's forests, which absorb carbon dioxide; and on reducing the amount of energy produced in the first place, through improved energy conservation and efficiency.

**The design decision**

Opportunities exist for scientists and designers to design products and buildings powered by alternative sources of energy, but perhaps the single most important theme for design generally is energy efficiency. Jug kettles are more energy-efficient than the kettles they replace, because they can boil smaller amounts of water safely. Products designed to run on batteries use far more energy than those which use mains electricty, although clearly there are times when mains electricity would not be available or convenient.

The energy efficiency of the production process is important, too. Different mills making the same paper may use energy with very different efficiency. Up-to-date technology may lead to improved energy efficiency. The amount of energy used to manufacture different materials varies widely. Aluminium uses up huge quantities of energy, but can subsequently

➤ Tram belonging to the Tramway de l'Agglomération Grenobloise (TAG) in France. The system was inaugurated in 1983 to help reduce congestion in Grenoble and revitalise the city centre; trams run on electricity and therefore help to reduce the pollution from petrol exhaust. These have been designed to high ergonomic, safety and comfort standards, and provide easy access for people in wheelchairs. Their introduction has significantly improved the quality of life in the centre of Grenoble.

be recycled several times, with low energy costs. Plastics are also energy-intensive to manufacture, but this energy is lost unless they are recycled or used in schemes that generate heat from waste.

Designers can play a role in conserving energy in several different ways:

- By designing products with improved energy efficiency.

- By designing products for recyclability. The energy required to manufacture a material originally is almost always greater than that required to recycle it.

- By specifying materials which have been produced efficiently. Many packaging manufacturers are now providing details of the energy cost of different materials.

- By using insulation materials, or solar panels, together with construction techniques that harness the warmth of the earth. This can dramatically reduce the energy requirements of buildings.

- By redesigning machinery and processes to reduce energy loss and to save production costs at the same time. Many industrial processes waste energy, simply because no one has really given energy efficiency a high priority.

- By encouraging more people to use public transport, through the design of attractive, convenient systems which can make people less dependent upon private cars.

## The ozone layer

Ozone occurring in the stratosphere, the zone 12 to 50 km above the surface of the earth, forms a protective shield against ultraviolet radiation from the sun. If the ozone layer thins or breaks, more ultraviolet rays will reach the earth's surface, causing damage to living substances, such as skin cancer in humans. Increased UV rays may also cause changes to the climate and to the ecosystem generally.

Ozone in the atmosphere is broken down naturally by UV rays, but this process is accelerated by the presence of chlorine, which destroys ozone molecules. Chlorine is released into the atmosphere by the breakdown of chlorofluorocarbons (CFCs). CFCs are used as blowing agents for plastic foams such as insulation and packaging materials; as refrigerants; as propellants in aerosol sprays, and as solvents for cleaning electronic components.

In addition to destroying ozone, CFCs are highly powerful greenhouse gases. Some of the alternative products proposed, such as hydrochlorofluorocarbons (HCFCs) and halon, also cause problems. Manufacturers of CFCs are developing more alternatives, because there is international agreement on the necessity first to freeze consumption of CFCs as soon as possible, and then rapidly to reduce it.

### The design decision

There are very few cases where CFCs are essential, and the designer should ensure that they are not specified. Alternatives exist for almost every use.

- In packaging, companies such as McDonalds have stopped using cartons made from CFC-blown foam, and most egg cartons and meat trays are now made of alternative materials. No material made using CFCs need be used in packaging, as satisfactory alternatives exist.

● Alternative propellants exist for aerosol sprays, but it is better to avoid aerosols altogether, as they represent a very high packaging cost and cannot yet be safely recycled. Pump sprays are a suitable alternative for most applications, although some medical uses require the precision and fine droplet delivery that currently only aerosols can provide.

● Alternative insulation materials are being developed, including one that uses waste paper.

● In refrigeration and air-conditioning, a variety of alternatives are being tested.

It would be inadvisable to design any new product now that relied on CFCs, as legislation surrounding the control of CFC disposal is likely to get tougher. At the moment, products which do use CFCs, such as refrigerators, should be designed so that they can be collected again after use, and the CFCs carefully drained and re-used.

## Tropical deforestation

Between the early 1960s and the mid-Eighties, three quarters of a billion acres

of forest were lost. Forests in temperate regions are relatively stable, although many trees are dying due to the effects of air pollution. The main cause for concern is the rate of destruction of the tropical rainforest. If the current rate continues, it is estimated that all rainforests will have disappeared within eighty years.

The effects of deforestation include the destruction of species, since rainforests contain a wide diversity of animal and plant life, most of it unique; the disruption of local climates, possibly leading to desertification due to changes in rainfall patterns; desertification, and the loss of habitat for local people. The destruction of vast areas of forest is also considered to be a significant contributory factor in the

▲ ▼ Acid rain is caused when coal or oil is burned, releasing sulphur and nitrogen into the atmosphere. These pollutants combine with water in clouds and eventually fall as rain, snow or mist, often long distances away from their source. Over half of Germany's forests are thought to be dying or dead as a result of acid rain damage, and many historic buildings are literally being eaten away. The *Guide to Tree Damage* was designed by Gary Rowland Associates for the World Wildlife Fund.

▼ In 1990 the UK-based Habitat furniture retailing company introduced a range of garden furniture and accessories made from rattan, sourced mainly from sustainable plantations in Indonesia. This is part of an initiative in rainforest management, to identify crops which can be extracted without harming the forest. In 1989 Habitat stopped selling any furniture made from tropical hardwoods such as mahogany.

greenhouse effect and brings about global climate change, as forests act as absorbers of carbon dioxide.

Tropical deforestation is caused by a variety of factors. Population growth forces people to try to cultivate forested land; fuel is required to support the population's energy requirements; commercial logging is an essential generator of foreign currency in many countries and, in large areas of Southern America, cattle ranching has caused the destruction of rainforests.

**The design decision**

The strong demand in Europe, North America and Japan for tropical hardwoods is met by forestry practices which are not sustainable. A few companies claim to replant, and to cut down only a small proportion of trees, but the vast majority of felled timber results in loss of irreplaceable forest. Many species have become extinct and many more are now endangered.

Tropical hardwoods tend to be associated with high-value end-uses, such as furniture, musical instruments and durable boards for exterior protection of buildings. A great deal of it, however, is used for chipboard, plywood and window

frames, and in other areas where other woods, or different materials altogether, would be entirely appropriate.

The simple design decision is not to specify any tropical woods, unless it can be proved that they are produced in a sustainable way. Timber merchants should be able to supply that information, and all reputable merchants should now be able to recommend and supply good alternatives for traditional tropical hardwoods.

However, the problem remains of providing a livelihood, and foreign currency, for the countries where the rainforests are situated. It has been estimated that the value of the raw materials in rainforests - nuts, fruits, medicinal plants, natural ingredients for foods and toiletries - would, if properly cultivated, far exceed the once-off value of the trees. The development of these raw materials is only just beginning. Pharmaceutical companies, and recently the UK-based cosmetics company The Body Shop, are seeking new active ingredients for drugs and cosmetics. Other substances may emerge which offer interesting potential to designers - natural dyes, for example, or leaves which can be used in the production of fine paper or packaging material.

▲ In North India, papermakers use chapri, a paper mould made from grass stems strung together, which gives the paper its characteristic laid pattern.

▼ In South India, papers are made from cotton rags mixed with tropical crop waste. Gunny papers are made from recycled jute sacking; banana paper from banana leaf fibre, and bagasse paper from sugar cane fibre. Other ingredients include rice husks, tea leaves, wool fibres and strings of algae. The papers here are being sorted before pressing, after which they are hung to dry.

▲ In Nepal, the lofka fibre - from the bark of a Himalayan plant - is used to make "washi" paper using a Japanese method. The lifted frame is seen with the wet sheet on its surface; this is peeled off when it has dried in the sun.

Handmade papers are produced in India using simple, low-cost equipment and local labour skills, but incorporating new techniques and materials. Sheet paper is formed by pouring a mixture of water and pulp into a mould: the water allows the pulp to spread evenly over the mould.

➤ Mountains of rubbish buried under the soil in landfill sites can be unstable and dangerous because of chemical reactions that occur as materials decompose. Dangerous substances may also leach out of unlined sites into the soil, eventually seeping out into the water supply.

◄ Fertilisers that drain into rivers and seas can stimulate the excessive growth of algae, which can be toxic to marine life. Toxic chemicals and sewage sludge are dumped directly into the sea, threatening wildlife and humans.

## Waste

The developed countries produce a billion tonnes of industrial waste each year, with the average household producing up to one tonne in household waste. Most of this ends up in landfill sites, some is incinerated, and some is simply dumped at sea. Each of these primary disposal methods has serious drawbacks, besides being a waste of valuable and often irreplaceable natural resources.

### Landfill

In many areas, such as the North East coast of the USA, space for landfill sites is simply running out. Existing sites are full, and there is no room to create more, especially as no one wants a site near their home. Rubbish is often transported long distances to less heavily populated areas.

Rubbish deposited in landfill sites does not simply biodegrade into harmless substances, which become assimilated into the soil. Excavations of landfill sites have shown that even materials considered to be fully biodegradable, such as newspapers, do not decompose much in the airless atmosphere of most landfill sites.

Material in landfill sites often contains contaminants, such as metals or toxic chemicals, that eventually leach out into the surrounding soil, and then into rivers and streams, and end up in the water supply. The gases created by the decomposition of organic material contribute to the greenhouse gases, unless they are tapped and used for heating.

### Incineration

Burning rubbish can generate energy, although the energy needs to be used close to the source, or it is wasted.

Because of the mixed nature of waste, and the types of materials included in it, incineration can release toxic gases into the air unless a very high temperature is reached. Plastics and chemicals such as pesticides can give off dioxins, one of the most toxic substances known.

Incineration also leaves behind a residue which can contain dangerous metal pollutants; this then has to be disposed of in special sites.

### Dumping

Depositing rubbish out at sea may solve an immediate problem, but there is increasing evidence that it causes damage to marine life, and that there is a real limit on how much can be absorbed and safely broken down by the sea.

### The design decision

The most effective way of addressing the waste disposal problem is to produce less waste. This is an area where designers will have a crucial role to play, and where good design can really make a difference.

### Increase in the life of a product

Products can be made more durable, or easier to repair. Often, however, a product is intended to last only for a specified period of time because of the rapid advance of new technology which quickly makes it obsolete, or because the desired

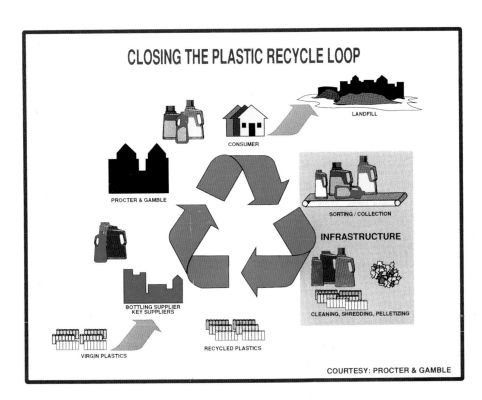

◄ Some types of plastic can be used several times. For example, soft drink bottles can be used as raw material for the manufacture of detergent bottles. Extending the life of plastic makes better use of a valuable resource, but the collection and separation of plastic waste demands an effective waste management infrastructure.

▼ ➤ Sanara shampoo bottles by Wella made from Biopol, a degradable plastic made from the fermentation of sugars, introduced by ICI in 1990. On disposal, Biopol is broken down by bacteria into carbon dioxide and water in the same way as other organic matter. In use, however, it is durable, stable and water-resistant. It may be appropriate for use in products which are disposed of via the sewage system, or composting, where recycling or re-use is not possible.

market rate of growth can be achieved only by a high level of replacement purchasing. Consumer attitudes to new features and styles may change, and resistance may build up to short-life products, making it easier for manufacturers to build to last. The Swedish car manufacturers Volvo are beginning to make a virtue out of the consistency of their car styles. They claim that they never risk being out of fashion, because the designs of their most popular models hardly change over time, so that, with the cars remaining in such good condition, people find it hard to tell how old they are. Where there is a real reason to update models (as

in the case of introducing energy-efficient appliances), designing for re-manufacture or recyclability in the first place can help minimise waste.

*Reduction in the amount of materials used*
Efficient use of materials, and imaginative component configuration or fabric pattern design, can reduce waste, as can miniaturisation. However, these moves, often inspired by cost-saving, can have a negative effect on the attractiveness of ultimate reclamation or recycling, because of the small amounts contained or because the reduction in the volume of materials has been accompanied by an increase in

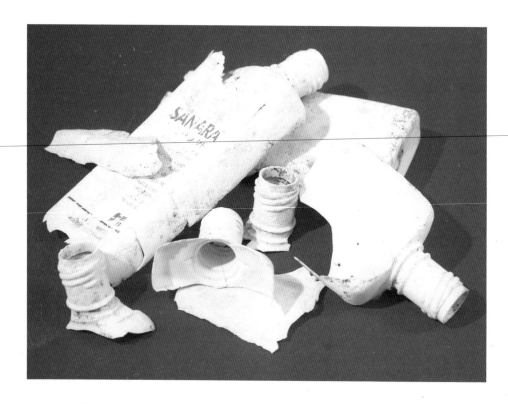

➤ Bottle banks and recycling bins can be large and unsightly. Busse Design in Ulm, Germany, have proposed this subterranean bottle bank, with an underground concrete container covered by a metal lid which can be walked on. The opening is easily accessible, and can form an attractive piece of street furniture.

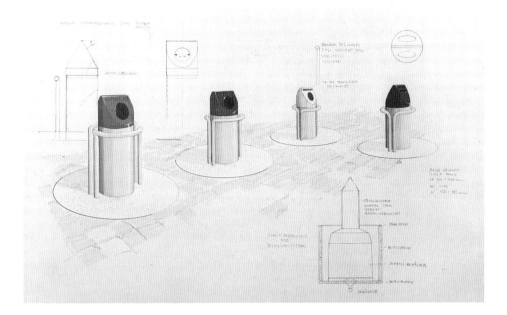

▼ Most breweries replaced the swingtop enclosure system years ago by the crown cap; however, it was retained by Grolsch, and is now a distinctive emblem. The top seal is recycled as well as the glass bottle, thus saving resources and reducing litter.

their variety and complexity. The move away from metals in automotive manufacture towards lightweight, easy-to-handle polymers reduced the attractiveness of the scrap car for the waste disposal industry. When choosing materials, therefore, and in particular when introducing a new material, designers should take into consideration the likely impact of that material on the eventual disposal or recovery of the product.

### Biodegradability of materials

Items which have to be disposed of, such as small components of surgical equipment, or products which consumers regard, wrongly, as disposable, such as pens or razors, might be manufactured from biodegradable material in the first place. This represents only a partial solution, as even biodegradable materials do not always biodegrade under landfill conditions. However, pens made out of paper may cause less of a problem and they certainly account for less waste than those made from plastic. Durability, rather than disposability, is the more appropriate longer-term solution, but this requires a significant change in consumer attitudes before it is acceptable.

Care must be taken about what happens to other components of the product. A cardboard camera introduced recently in Japan was severely criticised because of the risk that the batteries might be disposed of along with the camera; a special battery recyling scheme helped to make the product more acceptable.

Biodegradable plastics have caused much controversy. Early varieties, marketed as biodegradable, actually just disintegrated into fine particles of plastic,

which cannot be absorbed into the earth. However, later products, such as ICI's Biopol, are produced entirely from natural materials such as sugar, and break down into carbon dioxide. Plastic products which are disposed of into the sewage system could be made from this type of material, but biodegradable plastics cannot be introduced into a recycling stream.

### Re-use, recycling and re-manufacture

In areas such as packaging, re-use will become increasingly important, with the development of returnable packs and refill systems. The environmental choice between re-use and recycling depends on many different factors, including the type of collection and distribution infrastructure, the energy cost of cleaning for re-use versus heating for recycling, and the number of times a pack may be re-used. The same considerations apply to products and to construction materials.

Clearly, there is little point in designing a product for recyclability if there is no market for the recycled material, so one of the most important contributions designers can make is, where possible, to specify the use of recycled materials. The use of recycled paper is increasing steadily, but there has been little demand for recycled plastics. It is pressure from designers on plastics manufacturers that will above all encourage them to develop a wide range of useful materials from recycled plastic. In some applications, clearly, safety requirements may make the use of virgin materials necessary, but there are many applications where recycled material would be fine.

Some general guidelines apply to designing for recyclability:

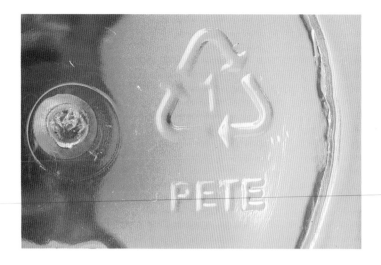

▲ Mark on the base of a soft drinks bottle identifying PETE, polyethylene terephthalate. More plastics will be identified in this way in future, to aid sorting for recycling.

● Make the components easy to disassemble.

● Reduce the number of different types of materials used.

● Avoid using combinations of materials which are not mutually compatible.

● Avoid composite materials where possible.

● Consider how materials can be identified (in the long term, some form of chemical tracing ingredients may be used).

● Ensure that it is possible to remove easily any components which would contaminate the recycling process (e.g. microprocessors).

For major items, like household appliances, industrial equipment, boats and furniture, re-manufacturing or refurbishment may be a more effective form of re-use. Restoring used items has only relatively recently become unfashionable in the developed world, and is still widely used in the Third World. Designing for re-manufacture involves:

● Ensuring that parts are interchangeable between items.

● Making components repairable, or easily replaced.

● Allowing for technological components to be replaced, without affecting the overall frame of the product.

● Choosing a classic, timeless exterior design, or allowing for the easy update of a style through the

replacement of a few key components such as panels.

Designing to minimise waste will require a good knowledge of the life cycle of the product, and good information about the performance of different materials within the re-use or recycling chain. It also raises fundamental questions about the wisdom of designing products which have a life expectancy far shorter than the life expectancy of the materials which go into making them.

## Water pollution

The growth in population and the increasing use of water for industrial purposes mean that there is insufficient supply of clean water to meet demand. Water courses in developed countries are polluted with sewage, nitrates, chemical cocktails seeping from landfill sites and industrial discharges. In addition to possible dangerous effects on the drinking water supply, water pollution creates major problems for wildlife and plants: many stretches of river in Northern Europe have "died" because of pollution.

Pressure is increasing for industry to aim for "closed loop" waste management systems where no harmful substances are emitted, but there are many processes that use very large volumes of water where cleaning it may not be practicable. The use of chlorine to bleach paper has been strongly criticised by environmentalists, and many paper mills are now moving away from chlorine towards hydrogen peroxide or other less polluting cleaning agents. Certain dyes, such as cadmium, may also cause harmful emissions, and many other dyes are considered not to be fully biodegradable.

### The design decision

Designers and engineers may play a significant role in the redesign of industrial processes to reduce the need for harmful emissions; the development of pollution-abatement equipment also offers a rapidly growing opportunity for design skills. However, there are ways in which all designers can help to reduce water pollution and ease the shortage of clean water:

● The record of suppliers of raw materials and components should be examined to ensure that their manufacturing processes are not unnecessarily polluting. As a minimum requirement, suppliers should be able to demonstrate that they have not contravened local legislation concerning emissions.

- The processes by which specific ingredients are manufactured should be questioned. Titanium dioxide, used in a wide variety of products including paints and toothpaste, can be produced in different ways, with varying degrees of polluting effect. Paper produced by mills which use chlorine bleach should be avoided, in favour of unbleached paper, or paper bleached using hydrogen peroxide.

- The impact of dyes should be considered. Are they fully biodegradable? Could they cause a local pollution problem during manufacture? Could there be a contamination problem if dyed products end up in landfill sites?

- Saving water will be as important in some regions as saving energy. Designers can aim to design household appliances which use far less water. Imaginative devices for collecting and using rainwater will also be required.

## Resource consumption

The conservation of natural resources and the responsible management of renewable resources lie at the heart of the concept of sustainable development, which will become an essential theme for politics and industry. The idea that we should aim to meet today's needs without harming the ability of future generations to meet their needs is a very simple one, but with fundamental implications. Using up non-renewable resources is an obvious concern, but simply increasing consumption of renewable resources may not be the solution.

The designer has an impact on this issue in three principal ways.

### Choice of materials

Materials may be natural or synthetic, recycled or virgin, renewable or non-renewable. There are no clear-cut answers about which is least environmentally damaging. Naturally occuring materials may be in very short supply, so that to produce all dyes from natural sources, for example, would require vast quantities of plants which would have to be grown somewhere, possibly replacing more valuable crops. Growing trees for harvest can cause disruption of local eco-systems and soil erosion, as in the case of eucalyptus trees planted outside their natural growing areas. The use of plastics contributes to the depletion of oil reserves, but plastics can help reduce the weight and therefore the fuel consumption of vehicles.

Despite these difficult trade-offs, and the need to examine each case individually, there are some general guidelines:

- Materials which occur near to their point of use have the advantage that they require less energy to transport. The use of locally occurring construction materials is also becoming increasingly popular among architects, as a way of helping

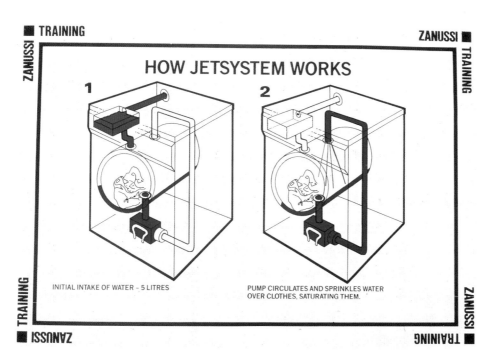

◄ The Zanussi Jetsystem washing machine assesses fabric type, weight and volume of load to allow dramatic savings of water and energy. The water is circulated to the top of the machine and sprinkled down on the clothes, to simulate the action of hand washing.

buildings to fit more comfortably into a location.

- Materials made from non-renewable resources should be re-usable or recyclable wherever possible.

- The extraction process of some raw materials, such as aluminium and gold, can cause severe damage to local habitats. While the designer cannot take responsibility for what happens at the very start of the supply chain, this is one area where information should be requested wherever possible from raw materials suppliers or intermediaries. Purchasing decisions should reflect a desire to support mining and extraction activities that cause the least damage.

- The specification of recycled and waste materials will very often be a sensible decision on both cost and environment grounds. Waste products such as steel, corrugated iron and driftwood have been used as materials for furniture and sculpture, and could find other high-value uses.

### Energy content

A second area where the designer can make a major impact on resource consumption is in considerations about the energy used throughout the chain of extraction, manufacture, transit, use and disposal. Guidelines for energy efficiency are outlined above.

| Environment issue \ Product life cycle | Supply | Production | Distribution | Use | Disposal |
|---|---|---|---|---|---|
| Waste | | | | | |
| Soil contamination | | | | | |
| Water contamination | | | | | |
| Air contamination | | | | | |
| Energy consumption | | | | | |
| Noise | | | | | |
| Local habitat | | | | | |

**Reduction in the need to consume**
Creating a fashion for minimalism is one approach, but another could be to design multi-purpose, highly functional products which, literally, reduce the number of objects, clothes or pieces of furniture one needs. Specific, single-purpose kitchen appliances could be replaced by machines which perform several different tasks.

## Noise

Although noise pollution is not a life-threatening or ecology-destroying environmental problem, it is an increasing source of discomfort to people. Major

▲ The cradle-to-grave approach requires analysis of a product's environment impact through each stage of its life. Charts such as this one prompt thought about every aspect of the life cycle; they are being used to assess products for eco-labelling schemes.

◄ A restrained use of materials is now common in exclusive fashion stores. At Junko Shimada in Paris, white walls and ceilings contrast with the black granite of the raised platform and the white granite of the floor.

improvements have been made in the reduction of the noise levels of many industrial machines, but noise can still be a real health hazard in some industries, particularly in heavy manufacturing. Noise from motor or air traffic is a serious problem for those living near to busy routes, and even the noise from domestic machines such as lawnmowers can cause considerable irritation and a real impairment of the quality of life.

### The design decision

The selection of raw materials, and the construction techniques used, can greatly affect the noise levels of a machine or building. Sometimes the use of lightweight materials can reduce noise output; increased insulation can absorb sound; improving the efficiency of a machine may make it less noisy. By pursuing other improvements in environment performance, noise output may also be improved as a side effect.

## The cradle-to-grave approach

Assessing the true environment impact of a product or construction can be done only if consideration is given to its effect throughout all the stages of its life. Focusing simply on its impact during use, or on one of its characteristics, such as recyclability or energy efficiency, gives only a partial and possibly misleading picture of its overall performance. The cradle-to-grave idea underlies the assessment systems developed for most official eco-labelling systems, and its use as a framework for product development and design can thus be expected to spread rapidly.

The cradle-to-grave approach acknowledges that environment issues may emerge at any stage, including raw material extraction; ingredients processing; manufacture or construction; distribution; use, and disposal.

The calculation of the exact impact overall may be almost impossible. Many research institutes and major manufacturers are attempting to develop objective eco-balance equations but, although it may be possible to measure energy consumption with some accuracy, other aspects of environment impact are harder to establish. Because there is no way yet of comparing different types of impact - water pollution and noise, for example - it is extremely difficult to make overall comparisons between different products with different environment profiles. For the moment, the cradle-to-grave form of assessment provides a useful framework and checklist for ensuring that every

aspect of the product is considered. For practical purposes, though, it may prove necessary to focus attention on a limited number of areas which cause the greatest potential environment impact, while ensuring that performance in all other areas meets certain standards.

▲ Interior of a house built into the rock on the cliffs of the Spanish island of Menorca. Designed by Javier Barba of Barcelona, it features naturally thick walls to keep out the heat, and local, natural materials for the interior (for more details, see pages 66-7).

◄ Lamp made from discarded computer boards in the shape of a Thirties skyscraper by British sculptor and clockmaker Philip Hardaker, a member of Reactivart, an environmental-based art group. The group re-uses obsolete objects, especially hi-tech and industrial products, and turns them into decorative and functional works of art. Computer boards, in particular, have a very short functional life, the ones used here being only a few years old.

# 3 Architecture and interior design

➤ From a distance, this house, designed by Javier Barba and built into a rocky cliff in Menorca, is almost invisible (for more details, see pages 66-7).

Buildings are responsible for more external pollution than any other product. About half the greenhouse gases produced each year by industrialised countries are related to buildings, through the use of energy. Buildings also contribute directly to other global environmental problems, such as acid rain and the reduction in the ozone layer. The impact on the local environment can be negative, too - disturbing local habitats, generating pollution, contaminating the soil and defacing the landscape. The way in which a building is designed and built is therefore extremely important.

The ability of architects or designers to influence environment impact is directly related to how early in the planning of the building they are involved, and whether the work is an entirely new building or a refurbishment. As with most issues in this area, the earlier that environmental criteria are considered the better.

Finding ways of minimising the harmful effects of buildings may lead in two apparently contradictory directions: the development of highly sophisticated technology to help control the functions inside a building; and the use of entirely natural, very simple features, to ensure that the building makes the best use of its site, and is comfortable and attractive to live in.

Decisions taken at the design stage of a building have long-term consequences because they determine how the building is serviced - i.e. lit, heated and ventilated. They also determine how well the building will fit into the local area and community. It is therefore important to conduct a thorough investigation of the proposed development even if it is one modest building rather than a major project, to ensure that all factors have been considered.

The architect and designer have a major role to play in determining how well the building will perform in terms of energy usage and human health and safety. They also have a role in promoting the use of materials which are produced in an environmentally sensitive way.

## Energy efficiency

Increasing the energy efficiency of buildings is one of the most significant areas of opportunity for energy conservation. Architects and designers can directly contribute to reducing the risk of the greenhouse effect by creating buildings which consume substantially less energy. Although it is not possible to control the human activity within buildings that may involve careless use of energy, the way in which the building is designed can moderate the use of energy without the occupants having to be particularly aware of it. Designing for energy efficiency involves an integrated approach, from building structure and internal systems right through to interior furnishing.

There are two broad approaches. The first aims to minimise the impact of the external environment, through the use of good insulation, controlled ventilation and economic use of space. The second is to use directly the effect of the sun and natural ventilation to minimise the need for heating and cooling systems. This approach uses the siting of the building as a major contributor to internal climate control. The different approaches will be appropriate in different situations. In each development, there has to be a balance between construction cost, technical feasibility, energy effectiveness and function.

▲ A major housing development in the UK, the Energy Park at Milton Keynes explores many different ideas that promote energy efficiency. The Spectrum 7 building, designed by The ECD Partnership in London, includes a well insulated roof which admits daylight; a front elevation fully glazed for solar gain; automatically controlled low energy lighting, and a water-cooled floor slab which functions as a summer cool store. This was one of 49 Project Monitor case studies coordinated and published by The ECD Partnership on behalf of Directorate-General XII of the Commission of the European Communities 1987-89 (see also pages 10-11, 42-3 and 156-7 ).

## Site analysis

The primary focus of site analysis is to ensure that the land is used efficiently, and that the building fits appropriately into the service infrastructure. The way in which a building is sited, however, relative to other buildings or to natural features of the landscape, can be a major determinant of its energy efficiency. In a climate where protection is needed from cold, the building can take advantage of natural shelter such as trees or banks. Windbreaks, in the form of trees or walls, can prevent the area immediately surrounding the building from becoming as cold as it might do if unprotected from the wind; the outside of the house, therefore, does not become so cold, reducing the need for heating inside. However, in a hot climate, it could be important to ensure that the prevailing breeze can blow easily through the building, creating a natural cooling ventilation. In cities, the position of surrounding buildings is important, as this can determine the flow of wind currents, and therefore the temperature.

By making most use of naturally occurring climatic regulators, it is possible to reduce the degree of dependence on artificial forms of heating, cooling and ventilation. A study of the site, in terms of natural features, wind direction and positioning of other buildings, will build up a picture of the local climate, and how its features might be exploited or protected against.

## Solar design

The use of solar power as a source of energy is not simply confined to countries with long hours of sunshine. Houses can be designed to capture and store solar energy, and this can make a worthwhile contribution to heating requirements even in very northerly climates.

Solar power can be actively collected by the use of solar panels which absorb heat; alternatively, the house can be designed so that the structure of the house itself passively absorbs heat because of the nature of the materials it is made from.

### Active solar heating systems

First the sun heats metal solar panels on a sun-facing roof. The heat is then collected by circulating either air or water around the hot panels. Air is passed into a thermal store such as a rock bed, before being distributed round the building through ducts with the help of fans. Water is stored in a tank, for use directly as hot water, or is circulated in pipes to provide radiated heat.

Solar panels are becoming a regular feature of new buildings, easily incor-

➤ ⩒ This abandoned stone quarry in Barcelona has been transformed into a public park by architects Martorell Bohigas and Mackay in collaboration with A. Martinez. La Crueta del Col Park was completed in 1989. The north slope was reforested, with facilities for picnics and an open-air theatre; terraces on the edge of the hillside provide sports areas. On the south side is a 100-metre wide lake, with a series of steps and terraces leading up to the rim of the crater. A gangway follows the crater rim, and sculptures add extra interest.

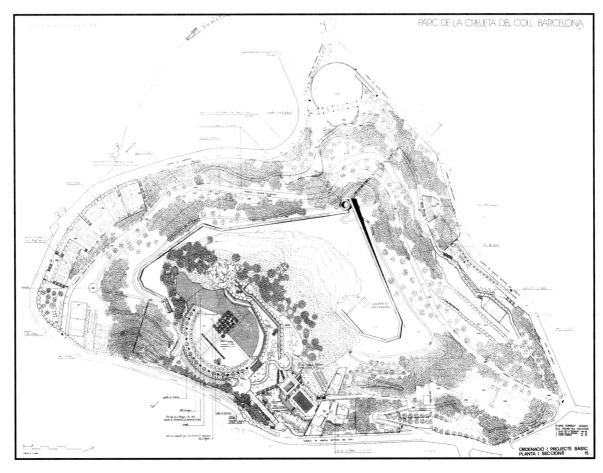

porated and aesthetically acceptable. The costs of installing them, however, can mean that the cost-saving payback is achieved only in the longer term, as the initial cost of materials and installation is relatively high.

*Passive solar heating systems*
Potentially, these offer a low-cost approach to the use of solar power, as the heating system effectively runs itself without the use of mechanical components. The sun warms the building directly through the windows, and the walls and floors act as heat absorbers; they store the heat until the air has cooled sufficiently to cause it to flow naturally out again.

Windows designed to capture heat effectively have to be large and south-facing, to ensure that more heat is trapped than lost. A conservatory or glass-covered balcony will increase the amount of solar energy collected: it will heat up quicker than the rest of the building, so warm air from it will flow through the rest of the building. During cool periods, the warm air left in the conservatory insulates the area of the building to which it is attached, and thus helps preserve the temperature inside. Large areas of window can be covered during the night by shutters, to prevent heat being lost through the glass. Reflective blinds can also be helpful in regulating temperature.

The heat let in through the windows must be absorbed by the walls and floors, which should be made of stone, brick, concrete, even earth. The thicker and more solid the floors and walls, the better they are likely to be at thermal storage. Thin board and carpets do not work in the same way. However, modern lightweight materials can be made more effective in thermal storage by "reinforcing" them with thick ceramic tiles or plaster. In addition, dark surfaces absorb the sun's heat considerably more than light ones.

Walls can be specially constructed to make them even more effective energy-storers. Walls made out of stone or brick, covered in special glass or glaze, can be used on the sides of the building most exposed to the sun; the heat absorbed can be circulated, in the form of warm air, throughout the building. Another approach is to use walls containing water, which is a most effective heat store. Water columns or water walls can either be hidden or used to provide an interesting design feature.

▼ ➤ The ten-storey Orbassano apartment block in Turin, Italy, was commissioned by the Unione Piemontese Svilieppo Edilizo as part of a programme of solar heating and low energy schemes, which was used as a case study for the EC's Project Monitor (see page 40). The tower, a right-angled triangle with the angle trimmed off at 45 degrees, has two fully glazed sides facing south-east and south-west. All forty apartments have full-width "sunspaces" adjacent to the main living rooms, which are single-glazed to allow the heat to penetrate, and which have concrete floors to provide thermal mass for heat storage. Solar panels which heat the air supply nearly half the annual hot water demand and contribute to space heating, while high levels of insulation minimise heat loss. The heat requirements from other sources are only half those of similar blocks.

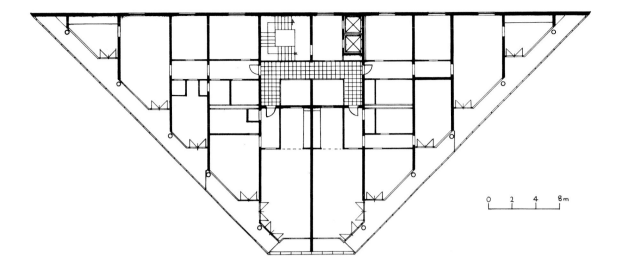

One indirect way of using solar energy is to make use of earth as a good moderator of temperature, and take advantage of the fact that it takes a long time to heat up and cool down. Building a house below the soil, or covering it partially with a layer of earth and grass, will help keep it warmer in winter and cooler in summer.

### Heating systems

More effective insulation, and the use, for example, of passive solar heating, will help reduce the demand for large heating systems, but in most buildings there will still be a need for a source of heat which can be precisely controlled. Simply designing a system which can be flexible enough to allow for a variety of different temperatures can significantly improve energy efficiency.

It may be efficient for large buildings to have their own system for generating heat and power. Combined heat and power can reduce the amount of energy needed in heating the building. Gas can be used to fuel a boiler which generates electricity. The electricity is used in the building, while the hot water from the engine's cooling circuit can be circulated in the heating system, or used simply as a direct hot water supply.

### Lighting and appliances

These features are often not regarded as an integral part of the building, but as the province of the interior designer. But both are major energy consumers, and offer opportunities for savings.

Lighting should be considered as a total system, where the aim is to develop the most appropriate combination of natural light and artificial light. Although as much natural light as possible is desirable, this might lead to too much sunlight and heat at times, unless it is possible to shade the windows effectively. The use of vast expanses of glass in modern office buildings often simply makes it necessary to have an air-conditioning system. Many new developments in glass aim to allow maximum daylight while keeping out excessive heat.

While it may be possible to supply most daytime lighting needs from natural light, electric light will of course be needed during the night, and for localised, more intense lighting requirements.

About half of the energy used in lighting is wasted. Incandescent light bulbs, the sort most commonly used, give off most of the energy they use as heat, not light. Energy consumption in lighting can be reduced by the use of longer-life, more efficient lamps. Changing from tungsten incandescent lamps to fluorescent lamps can reduce the amount of energy used by a factor of at least five. Modern fluorescents with high frequency ballasts minimise flickering and the problems of eye strain associated with it. Halogen lamps can also offer considerable energy savings, and can give a lighting effect that is very close to daylight.

### Building materials

Designing for energy efficiency must also take into account the amount of energy that has been used in the manufacture of the building materials. There is little point improving the energy efficiency of a building if the materials needed to achieve this required more energy to make them than would be saved during the building's lifetime. Fortunately, many of the most energy-efficient materials, such as stone, are natural, and not highly energy-intensive to extract and use, unless they are transported over long distances.

▲ The Parachute fashion store in New York, designed by Harry Parness, uses simple, rough materials and fittings to create a humorous, original effect. Wooden football benches, a painted concrete floor and original cast iron columns provide the backdrop, while recycled packing cartons and simple wire hangers form the display.

Sophisticated forms of thermal glass, however, although energy-intensive to produce, will justify their energy cost through subsequent savings.

Double glazing is a simple form of insulation, which can be highly effective. New designs are now incorporating special mirrors, which reflect back over-powerful summer sun, while allowing winter sun to penetrate the glass. Coatings can make it possible for light to enter the building, but not pass out again.

Well insulated walls have traditionally been one of the major elements of designing for energy efficiency. Cavity walls, filled with heat-absorbent insulation material, can be extremely effective, although care must be taken with the choice of insulating material to avoid foams manufactured with CFCs.

## "Intelligent" building controls

"Intelligent" building controls allow heating, lighting and appliances to be switched on and regulated as needed, with the aim of using the minimum energy. Sensitive thermostats and light sensors, combined with a computer-based programme, allow temperatures to be monitored and heating needs adjusted accordingly. For example, pre-selected heaters will be activated for frost protection during the winter; water heating can be precisely controlled to meet occupants' requirements. Most automated systems will aim to achieve maximum energy savings, but they allow the flexibility of overriding programmes to ensure convenience and comfort.

Control systems are becoming increasingly sophisticated. They no longer monitor one service only, such as heating, but can now provide a comprehensive and integrated approach to regulating the entire internal requirements and energy needs of the building.

## Ventilation and air-conditioning

Air-conditioning systems are major consumers of energy, in addition to being a potential source of hazardous CFC emission. The growth in their usage could offset the energy savings being achieved by more efficient use of lighting and heating. Pressures to install air-conditioning units may well increase further, in anticipation of the effects of global warming. It is therefore important to consider how they could be made more efficient, and also whether any viable alternatives exist.

◀ At Issey Miyake in London, designed by Armstrong Chipperfield in 1985, natural materials were used to produce a timeless, quality feel. Contrasting materials were used to define separate areas within the store - black slate, Portland stone and white marble.

The use of "intelligent" controls will help reduce energy wastage but, from a design perspective, it is worth considering how the structure of a building can help to keep it cool, reducing the need for any artificial cooling.

Just as solar energy can be used to heat thermal stores to provide a source of heating for a building, so thermal stores can be used to help cool a building. Heat collected during the day is radiated off to the outside during the night, enabling the store to absorb the next day's heat. Solar energy can also be used to power refrigeration units, and so can provide a complete approach to heating and cooling; there is usually, however, a need to supplement the system with a complementary one, because of the unpredictability of weather.

Alternatives to air-conditioning may lie in the use of natural ventilation systems. A natural flow of air is created through a building because of the differences in pressure between cold and warm air. On the windy side of a building air will be cooler, and will flow towards the low-pressure side of the building away from the wind, displacing warmer air. Warm air will be lost upwards, through chimneys, for example, while cooler air is drawn in at a lower level. This form of natural ventilation creates a through draught of cooler air, and also allows moisture to escape.

Up until recently, most buildings were naturally ventilated, because construction techniques left many gaps through which air could leak. However, warm air lost in

▲ ▼ The experimental workshop at Hooke Park College, UK, for the furniture designer John Makepeace applies sophisticated technology and engineering skills to roundwood - timber with a trunk diameter of 50-200 mm - which traditionally has been used only for low-quality applications. Instead of a post-and-lintel construction, the length of roundwood timbers and their flexibility when wet have been exploited. The trees are debarked, treated with preservative, and then bent into place. The shell action of the three-dimensional frame reduces the bending stresses. The shells are covered by a polymer membrane roof, with insulation sandwiched between; the membrane is both the ceiling of the workshop and the diagonal bracing to the shells. Computer analysis was used to establish the shape and predict the stresses as the bending took place.

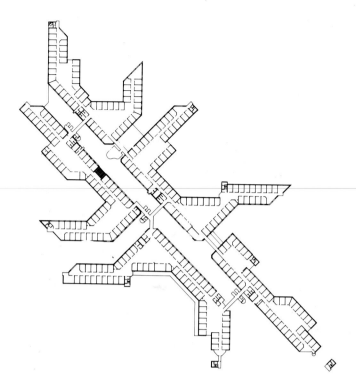

▲ The headquarters of Scandinavian Airlines at Frosundavik, near Stockholm, was designed by Niels Tomp. One of the aims was to create a working environment that would be free from "sick building syndrome". Almost all of the 1,500 employees working in the building have their own daylit room, with individual controls for lighting and heat. Windows look either to the outside or to a central atrium.

this way also represents a loss of energy, and so the challenge is now to retain the benefits of natural ventilation without the associated heat loss. The use of mechanically controlled ventilation, incorporating a heat recovery unit, can capture lost heat while ensuring that condensation problems are minimised.

## Material specification

Architects and designers have a considerable opportunity to influence environment impact through the specification of materials. Understanding the environment issues surrounding the extraction of raw materials, the manufacture of construction materials, and their effects in use, is important to ensure that environment problems are minimised.

### Natural materials
The general principle of using, wherever possible, non-toxic materials which are produced from renewable or re-usable resources can be taken as a guideline.

Wood is the obvious material in this respect, but it is not suitable in all applications. Opportunities may well exist for the incorporation into construction materials and fittings of new materials made from waste products such as paper and plastics. The selection of recycled materials has to depend on the performance requirements demanded, but could be significantly increased. The construction and furniture industries are major potential users of recycled plastics, and designers should

aim to specify these in preference to virgin plastic wherever possible.

The selection of materials is of course determined to a considerable degree by the overall building and design concept. Materials have to be considered in the context of heating, functional use and appearance.

### Timber choice
The use of tropical hardwoods in the building industry has been strongly criticised by environmentalists. Tropical timber is often used in building joinery, for front doors and in window-frames. As most timber production is not carried out sustainably, its use contributes to the problems of deforestation, even though most deforestation is caused by the burning of forest to clear land for homes and agriculture. Tropical hardwoods, valued for their strength and appearance, have been used in applications such as plywoods and chipboard, where other materials would be just as appropriate.

Designers and architects specifying timber are now encouraged to avoid using tropical hardwood products altogether, unless it is possible to determine that the timber has originated from one of the few sustainably managed forests. Temperate hardwoods, such as cherry and alder, might be used instead; alternatively, softwoods may be suitable for some applications that have traditionally been reserved for hardwoods.

The use of hardwood veneers, as a way of greatly reducing the quantity of material used while still benefiting from its appearance, has attracted considerable controversy. The appeal of veneers has grown because it allows the use of low-grade softwood waste in place of solid wood, at a considerable cost saving. However, critics would claim that the veneer material must still come from a temperate hardwood or a sustainably managed tropical source.

### Local materials
The amount of energy used to transport building materials from their source to the building site can be a major consideration. The transport of large quantities of very heavy materials over long distances can represent a very inefficient use of resources, if there are materials available nearer to hand that would meet the requirements.

The use of locally occurring materials is becoming more popular because of the emphasis now being put in many planning considerations on how well the building fits in to the local environment.

### Chlorofluorocarbons

CFCs are used in rigid polyurethane and extruded polystyrene foams, often employed in insulating material. They are also used as refrigerants in air-conditioning systems, and in fire protection equipment. Architects and building contractors are now faced with the challenge of finding satisfactory alternatives in all these areas.

While some manufacturers of insulating foam have switched to using gases which are far less harmful than CFCs, others are using alternative products altogether, such as mineral fibre or densely packed waste paper material. The range of alternatives is increasing constantly, so it is important to keep up to date with developments through professional associations and trade magazines.

Alternatives to CFCs are also being developed for use in air-conditioning systems. From the architects' perspective, the first approach may well be to minimise the need for air-conditioning systems altogether, through the use of natural ventilation or shading. But if a refrigeration plant is necessary, it is now possible to design the system to operate on refrigerants which are significantly less damaging than CFCs. Currently, R22 is being used, but many others are in development. Again, this is an area where it is important to work closely with suppliers to ensure that state-of-the-art systems are incorporated wherever possible. Poor design and maintenance of air-conditioning systems have been a major problem in the past,

resulting in leakage of CFCs. Consideration must therefore be given, when designing and installing a system, to ensuring easy access for checking.

### Hazardous materials

The potentially dangerous side effects of materials commonly used in construction, decoration and furnishing have recently become a cause of concern. The carcinogenic effect of asbestos has led to its removal from many buildings, and to prohibition of its use in some countries. The use of lead in paints is being reduced or abandoned, because of the dangers it can cause to children if ingested.

However, concern is now being expressed across a much wider range of substances. Many of the modern products taken for granted in building and decoration - such as formaldehyde, epoxy and acrylic resins, and fungicides - are criticised not just for the pollution caused by their manufacture, but also because of concern that they can act as allergens, causing conditions such as asthma, hay fever and skin problems.

As with so many environmental issues, trade-offs have to be evaluated. The use of chipboards made from waste materials offers many benefits, but the glues in the manufacturing process can be toxic in production and use. Products are becoming available with a low formaldehyde content, and these should be specified in preference. Timber is frequently treated with pesticides and fungicides designed to protect the wood from infestation and rot.

▲ The residence of Leif Nørgaard (who runs Novotex, see pages 146-7), in central Jutland, Denmark, designed by Jørgen Johansen. Difficult to spot in the landscape, its shape and situation mirror the lines of the land, and its structure is low to avoid being obtrusive. The roof is covered by a thin layer of grass for further concealment. The open-plan house faces south, with large windows to provide passive solar heating.

The chemicals used, and their quantities, can result in toxic fumes which are dangerous to human health for some time, and there is pressure to ensure that chemicals banned in all other situations are not used in the building industry. The selection of appropriate materials, and the design of effective ventilation systems, can reduce the need for protection with large quantities of chemicals.

Good ventilation will reduce the risk to human health of emissions of toxic chemicals from furniture, construction materials and paints. Water-based paints, and paints made from plant materials, offer alternatives to the traditional resin-based paints, although they do not always provide the same level of protection.

There has been a recent increase in the tendency to relate ill health to buildings. "Sick building syndrome" is a term applied to a range of symptoms, including headaches, congestion and lethargy. Flickering fluorescent lighting, poor ventilation and low humidity have been blamed, and there is evidence to suggest that the incidence of these problems is lower where people can control their immediate environment, rather than have to rely totally on sealed systems.

Designers and architects can help reduce risks to human health through care in the specification of materials, minimising the use of toxic chemicals, ensuring good indoor air quality and temperature control, and selecting appropriate, flicker-free lighting systems, with lighting positioned to meet users' specific tasks. Large quantities of plants in offices and homes can have a beneficial effect on the atmosphere, helping to maintain the quality of the air, in addition to contributing to the aesthetic appeal of the building. However, the use of insecticides must be strictly controlled.

There is some evidence to suggest that radon, a naturally occurring radioactive gas produced by the decay of uranium in the soil, can accumulate into high concentrations in buildings located near a source. Assessments are now beginning to be made of soil conditions to try to detect the presence of radon, and steps can be taken to prevent its accumulation. Special floor linings or fan systems may offer some protection.

◄ ► Architect Gustav Peichl has succeeded in concealing much of the building development which accompanies this telecommunications satellite dish in Aflenz, Austria. The objective was to minimise disturbance to the landscape by locating offices and houses under the ground. The circular designs mirror the shape of the satellite dish to create a harmonious blend of technology and nature; from down the hill, the development is well concealed. Rooms are positioned around central holes in the ground which form courtyards lit by natural light.

## Town planning and countryside protection

It is beyond the scope of this book to address in any detail the important area of urban design; clearly, the environment impact of a building cannot be considered in isolation from its surroundings. Many major advances have been made in the design of large urban areas, with the aim of improving the quality of life for their inhabitants, as well as encouraging efficient use of energy, good public transport systems and street layouts which are appropriate to climatic conditions. The zoning of buildings can improve energy efficiently, for example by planning residential buildings in areas which can benefit from solar gain, while storage buildings or parking areas are located in areas receiving little sun.

Landscape design should be carefully considered at the planning stage of buildings. Often regarded as merely a cosmetic afterthought, landscape design can make a significant contribution to improving the environmental impact of a building or urban area.

Energy-conscious design requires careful analysis of the natural benefits and problems of a site, and the incorporation of features such as slopes, trees and hedges into the building plans. The increased use of large areas of trees is to be encouraged, not just for their visual appeal and protection properties, but also because of their ability to absorb carbon dioxide.

### Environment impact assessment

Many countries already have planning requirements which demand a formal assessment of the environment impact of any development at the planning stage. This is often confined to large developments which are proposed for conservation areas, but there is an increasing tendency for environment impact assessments to be regarded as part of "good practice" requirements from developers. Broadly, the assessment should consider the direct and indirect effects the development has on people, soil, water, landscape, air climate, wildlife, plantlife and cultural heritage.

The intrusiveness of a development, in terms of its visibility in the surrounding

▲ ▼ For the Paul Smith fashion shop in London, the original shop frontage was retained, and fixtures rescued from old stores were used for the inside. The traditional, warm effect is one benefit of an environmentally sensitive saving of resources.

landscape, is also a concern of environment impact assessments. Increasingly, attempts are being made to find imaginative ways of making buildings blend in with the surroundings – even, in some cases, to the point of complete invisibility.

Issues such as pollution, accessibility, density of development and disruption of local habitats are also included. Transport and communication requirements are being given increased attention in many countries, where the provision of adequate mass transport systems is regarded as a prerequisite for any major developments, in order to discourage dependence on private cars.

➤ When the fish market in London moved out of the city centre, the original nineteenth-century building in Billingsgate on the north bank of the Thames was threatened with demolition. After public protest, it was listed for protection. The architects Richard Rogers undertook a major refurbishment, combining the original exterior features with a modern, practical interior to equip the building for contemporary requirements.

Environment impact assessments are generally regarded as a "one-off" review, conducted at the planning stage. They should, however, be regarded as a regular activity, used to monitor whether the building or development does actually perform as predicted. How does the actual environment impact compare with the assessment made initially? Could improvements be made to it? Most importantly, reviewing performance after time can provide feedback to help the planning process in future design.

There is considerable debate still about the extent to which living and working areas should be integrated. Developments in technology now mean that many factories and offices are "clean" enough to be incorporated within housing developments. Reduced travelling distances between work and home give obvious environmental benefits. The growth in tele-commuting may also affect people's work and leisure requirements.

## Re-use of existing buildings

The use of an existing building, in place of the construction of a new building, can lead to obvious environmental benefits. Energy can be saved, and existing materials used rather than wasted. The existing building may also have value aesthetically, or because it fits into the style of the surrounding area.

Recognition is growing of the environmental benefits of extending the life of an existing building, and of designing new buildings so that they will have an extended life. Flexibility of usage may have to be incorporated into original designs, or at least some anticipation of changing user requirements. For example, now that recycling has become widespread, private homes and offices need to be equipped with areas where materials can be segregated and stored for collection.

## A holistic approach

The Baubiologie - literally, "building biology" - movement which emerged in Germany in the mid-Seventies has been heralded as a new concept in architecture. Pioneered by Professor Anton Schneider, Baubiologie aims to design buildings with a healthy environment which promotes physical and spiritual well being through ensuring that the materials used cause minimal harm to the environment in their manufacture and use, and that they allow the house to "breathe". The house is likened to a living organism, with the same control and regulatory functions; the aim is to create a harmonious, balanced, self-sustaining environment which is relaxing and easy to live in. Baubiologie uses a scientific, rather than mystical, approach to determining materials use and layout, but sets out to influence life style, believing that environmental impact and health depend crucially on people's attitudes and way of life, rather than on purely technical considerations.

# *case study* *Simonds Farsons Cisk Brewery, Malta*

➤ Large windows on the north side allow daylight into the building without the risk of solar heat gain. The north vent chamber emerges from the roof, gaining height to encourage the stack-effect ventilation.

➤ Plan looking upwards through a ventilation chamber on the south side. The vents are shown open, as for night operation. Glazing roof lights admit diffused light during the day.

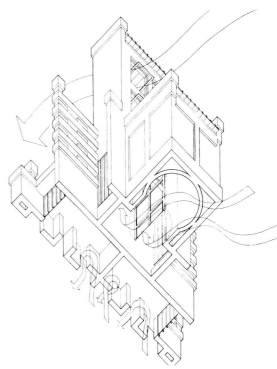

Buildings in the Mediterranean and Middle East have for centuries exploited the phenomenon of convective cooling. In Malta, traditional houses are made from local limestone, a stone with high thermal capacity which stores heat during the day. The internal temperature is regulated by shuttering the windows and by the massiveness of the stone. At night the shutters are opened, to draw in cool night air. This simple and highly effective approach has not often been reflected in contemporary architecture. Farsons Brewery, designed by Alan Short and Brian Ford of the UK architectural practice Peake, Short and Partners, relies on passive cooling systems to maintain the cool indoor temperature required for the brewing process. No air-conditioning is used.

The limestone building consists of a central core, the process hall, surrounded by a "jacket" of corridors through which air can circulate. Night ventilation occurs through a stack effect. Three towers high above the jacket provide exits for the circulating air. On summer nights, the temperature in the towers is higher than the temperature on the ground; as a result, cool air is drawn into the building. Vents into the process hall, opened at night, allow air to move through and remove the heat stored within the roof. The roof consists of a concrete deck with insulation on the upper surface. This "inverted" roof protects against solar heat gain during the day; its high thermal capacity provides a time-lag of several hours so that the peak internal temperature is not reached until well into the evening. By this time the night ventilation is already working to reduce it.

Maltese summers are characterised by a large diurnal range in temperature, and extreme heat can occur from time to time. The

➤ Very small glazed openings on the east side minimise solar heat gain, while vents in the wall supply air to the "jacket" space.

▲ A view of the roofline, showing the vents and roof lights standing above the roof plane.

effectiveness of the system was tested on a computer model, to predict how the building would react to typical and extreme weather conditions. Average August temperature in Malta is 33.3°C. The model predicted that the peak temperature in the brewery would be 25°C, rising above 27°C only on very extreme days. The brewery will therefore provide comfortable working conditions without the need for expensive air-conditioning.

In addition to saving energy through its ventilation system, the building also makes use of natural light through perimeter roof lights. To minimise solar heat gain, light entering the building is reflected off the jacket wall into the process hall.

The architects believe that the principles adopted for Farsons Brewery could be used on a wide range of industrial buildings.

▲ A view of the interior, looking to the north-west chamber, with the vents open. Ample light is provided from the large windows on the north side.

➤ The 12-metre high fermentation vessels in front of the south side.

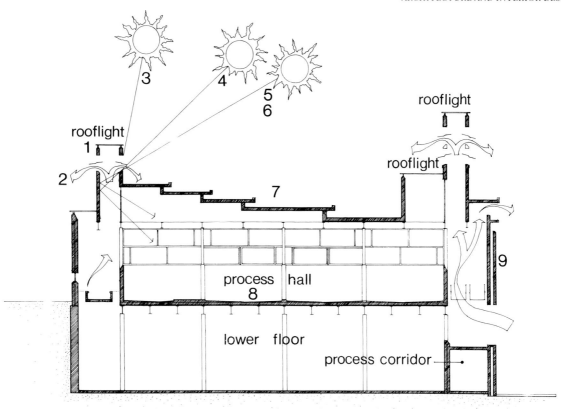

Diagrams showing the way the system works.

1   The process hall, indirectly lit from roof lights .
2   The "jacket", freely vented all day.
3   Temperature at noon on 21 June 25.5°C.
4   Temperature at noon on 21 October 6.1°C.
5   Temperature at noon on 21 December -1.1°C.
6   Low-altitude winter sun penetrates the building and is reflected from the back wall.
7   The roof mass provides a temperature time lag of about eight hours.
8   Predicted peak temperature 27°C.

9   The outer wall shades the inner wall, and the stack-induced air movement cools people on the walkways.
10  Air movement is encouraged by continuous slats on either side of the walkways.
11  Roof surfaces cool at night by radiation.
12  Interior surfaces cool convectively.
13  Tiled walls provide high thermal capacity.
14  Predicted minimum temperature 24°C.
15  Open volume allows cross ventilation.
16  Fresh air enters through "jacket" and into the lower floor.

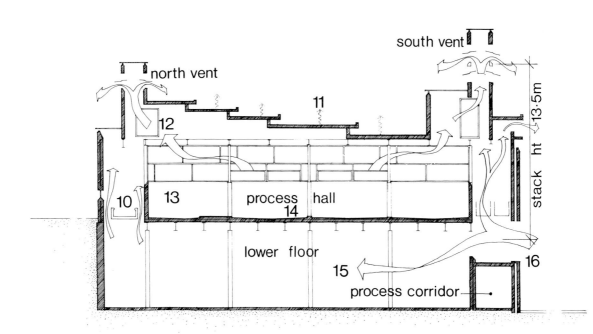

# *case study*  NMB Bank, The Netherlands

➤ **Broad staircases provide opportunities to meet, as well as encouraging fitness.**

The new corporate headquarters for NMB, the largest bank in The Netherlands, represents one of the most imaginative attempts at bringing together human and environmental concerns with those of flexibility, efficiency and low operating cost. A working environment has been created which is attractive and successful for its users.

Located in the south-east of Amsterdam, the bank has a dramatic appearance, externally and internally. Its walls slope, there is no air-conditioning in the conventional sense, and it contains a profusion of plants which are watered with purified rainwater fed from sculptures.

The building is the result of close collaboration between a team of engineers, landscape designers and architects, led by Amsterdam architects Alberts and Van Huut. Unusually, all the participants in the project were invited to contribute their ideas at the start, rather than being called in after the architects and clients had decided on the scheme. This allowed an integrated approach, where every element fitted sympathetically together.

The building is a series of towers, strung together in an "S" shape. Each has a different colour, providing distinct identities for different departments. Each floor of the tower houses between twenty and forty employees, giving an intimate feel to working areas. Noise from passing traffic is deflected by the sloping walls, which also deflect wind, so reducing the loss of heat from the building. The separate towers emphasise the organisational structure of the bank, but an interior street plays an important connecting role, and creates a common area: all the building's general services are along this street, as are restaurants and small shops. The street passes through a series of sunlit atria, open at all levels of the building.

Energy efficiency has been a high priority in the design and servicing of the building: it is considered to be one of the most energy-efficient in the world. There is no air-conditioning system, but rather a heat-recovery air-circulation system. Cool air is taken in during the night, passed through energy-transfer equipment and recirculated during the day; the concrete mass of the building is used as cold storage. Large solar energy collectors supply heat to supplement the gas-fired central heating system which provides about 80 per cent of power requirements. The windows on the south-facing walls also act as solar collectors, and the heat is taken to the shadow side of the building. Large water-tanks provide temporary heat storage, and the entire interior environment is regulated by a sophisticated computer.

Natural light is enhanced by the use of light-reflecting and dispersing materials in the window openings and work areas. Even though windows cover only 25 per cent of the wall surfaces, artifical light is needed during only 30 per cent of office time. Windows can be opened, to allow individuals to control their immediate temperature and ventilation.

Plants and gardens play a major role in the building, helping to give indoor areas an outdoor feel. The parking areas are covered with vegetation, and there are frequent views of the gardens

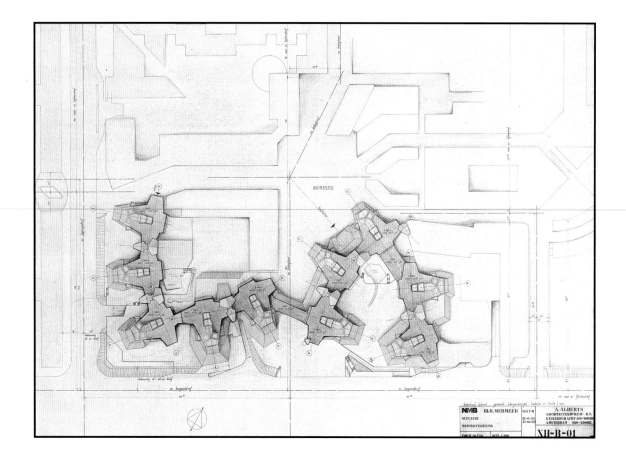

▲ Plan of the development, showing the series of towers which form an "S" shape. Each tower can have its own identity, but forms part of the whole chain.

from the central street. The extravagant use of the plants inside helps maintain a clean and pleasant atmosphere.

The central stairways are important features. Employees are encouraged to use the staircases rather than lifts for health reasons, but also to provide opportunities for social contact. The number of lifts was minimised, thus reducing construction costs.

Natural materials - such as wood, marble and copper - are used throughout the interior to create a warm effect. One notable feature is the lack of right-angled shapes: the architects believe that these discourage creativity and harmony, and therefore they have been avoided.

While the results of this design can be measured scientifically in terms of energy efficiency and noise levels, it is difficult to measure the impact of the building on employee health and satisfaction. One indicator, however, is given by the company: absentee rates have fallen, and prospective employees cite the new building as one of the major reasons for wishing to join the company.

◄ The unusual shapes and strong colours of the exterior of the NMB Bank create a dramatic effect. The sloping walls help to deflect wind.

# *case study*   *The Murphy house, USA*

▶ Entrance to the house, which is designed to promote harmony with the natural surroundings.

On the 35-acre semi-tropical Buck Island off the coast of South Carolina, USA, is a house designed for Jessica and Welles Murphy by Paul Bierman-Lytle of the Masters Corporation. The practice has pioneered the use of low-toxicity and non-chemically treated building materials, avoiding treated wallpaper, solvent-based glue and formaldehyde-based plywoods. Their aim is to ensure that closed living environments are as free as possible from any components which might be hazardous to the health of the user, producer or installer; that, wherever possible, renewable resources are used, and that waste products are biodegradable.

The Murphy house includes full-spectrum light bulbs, which are closer to natural light, and a heat-recovery ventilator that draws out stale air and brings in fresh. Insulation is derived from a mineral extracted from sea water.

◄ The dramatic spiral
staircase winding up to
the tower.

Vitreous tiles, linoleum, cork, stone, brick and solid wood are
the materials used for flooring and furniture. Decoration comes
from natural floor-coverings, such as cotton, wool or goat-hair
rugs over untreated jute. Synthetic wall-to-wall carpeting is
rejected because of concerns that it can harbour dust mites which
cause allergic reactions. Wood finishes are made from linseed oil,
citrus peel oil, juniper berries and rosemary.

The starting point for the design of the house was an appreci-
ation of the natural features and characteristics of the landscape
into which the house had to integrate. The luxurious tree-covered
appearance of the island is reflected in an indoor garden, while a
spiral staircase climbs up to a tower to afford spectacular views.

# *case study* *Thorsted Vest, Denmark*

➤ **Elevation showing the layout of the houses and the mix of built-up areas and open spaces which will give the town its spacious, country atmosphere.**

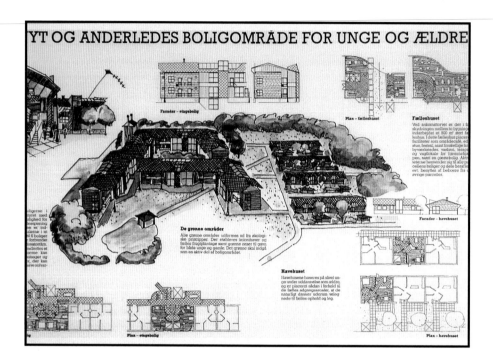

Ecological considerations have been given a high priority in the development of a new housing project on the outskirts of Horsens in Denmark. Eight to nine thousand houses, mixed with work and leisure spaces, are planned to extend the existing town. The work began in 1990, and will take shape over ten years, led by consultants Gruppen for by-og Landskabsplanlaegning a/s.

The basic principle used in planning the new development was to affect the balance of nature as little as possible, and to provide compensation for any damage caused. The aim is to provide a healthy environment, designed to meet the needs of the population, setting a positive relationship between town and countryside. Negative environment impacts, such as disturbing the water cycle or removing existing vegetation, will be balanced by positive improvements, such as providing new vegetation.

The development explores many different directions in the pursuit of good environment performance.

● Traffic
To reduce the impact of increased traffic, no through traffic will be allowed from the surrounding town, and low speed limits will be enforced. No traffic from industrial areas will be allowed into the housing areas, and paths will be given a high priority. The mixture of housing, work areas and leisure facilities is intended to reduce the need for transport, and an elaborate system of cycle paths will ensure that preference is given to cyclists and pedestrians. Recycled materials have been used for road construction, and the small roads will be coated with gravel to allow rainwater to be absorbed.

● Housing
The houses will use passive solar heating such as glass-covered verandahs to reduce energy consumption. Many are orientated south for solar gain, while shadows against southern elevations are avoided. Non-hazardous, environmentally considered building materials will be used, to create a healthy indoor climate. Extensive refuse treatment is planned: each house will include features to enable easy separation of different types of refuse, while organic waste will be composted. The separated waste will be delivered to gathering points, while large items will go to a central recycling cooperative where they may be repaired and re-used. Surplus waste which cannot be recycled will be used for combustion.

● Site design
The sites have been analysed for energy efficiency. Open, exposed areas will be protected from the wind by hedges, while the close and varied housing forms give good shelter. Lower parts of the development area will not be built upon, as they are subject to cold winds.

● Energy and water
Energy will be provided from a local power station fuelled by natural gas, and supplemented by solar and wind power. The consumption of water is minimised by using water-saving devices in household appliances; rainwater will also be collected and used.

● Open spaces
Large areas of open space will be created or preserved, with the aim of conserving and promoting local species of plant and animal life.

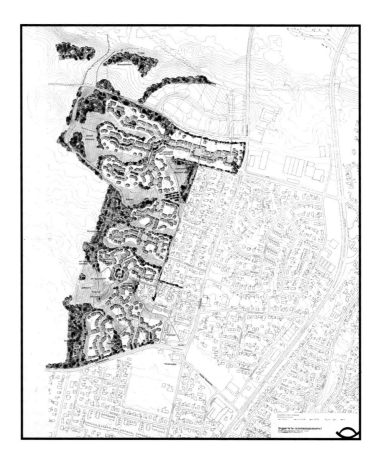

◄ The site plan of Thorsted Vest, showing the integration of housing and forest. The area is criss-crossed with winding paths.

# case study The Burghardt house, Germany

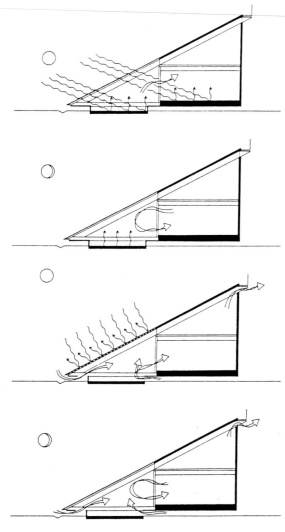

▲ Diagrammatic representation of the heat radiation and ventilation measures which contribute to the house's energy efficiency. From the top, the diagrams show winter day, winter night, summer day and summer night.

This private house in Regensburg designed by Thomas Herzog of Munich in 1979 demonstrates many of the principles of energy efficiency, the use of local materials, and the exploitation of site characteristics for protection and aesthetics. The plot is situated two metres below street level and is surrounded by high buildings, but the use of tall trees and a stream gives the feeling of being surrounded by a natural, rather than a city, environment.

The building is designed in a prismatic structure, on strict geometrical lines. The view of the surrounding buildings is deflected from the inside of the prism to the greenhouses which are integrated into the structure. These form one aspect of the passive solar gain heating system. The full range of energy-saving designs include:

● Insulating glass on the north, east and west walls to minimise heat loss.

● A south wall entirely glazed, with sliding doors to the conservatory area, which in the autumn and spring acts as a reservoir and in the winter as a buffer zone.

● The extensive use of wood as a construction material, helping to insulate against heat loss.

● A thick layer of insulating material in the floor, with a floor heating system at the top. Overheating is avoided by traverse ventilation through the gable walls, and the admission of cold air through slots.

The building requires only about 50 per cent of the energy needed by traditional houses of a comparable size.

The materials used in the construction were mainly locally sourced. Local wood features prominently, to give a warm and comfortable atmosphere. Small, unpolished limestone slabs were used for the flooring, with pieces chosen to correspond exactly to the cross-section of the timber supports, to avoid wastage.

It was the intention of the architect to expose the technical details of the construction as far as possible, and to use simple solutions which could be aesthetically attractive.

◄ View of the inside of the conservatory area, which functions as an intermediate temperature zone. It opens out to outside terraces which are sheltered by the indentation of the building.

➤ View from the south side, showing the large expanse of glass which contributes significantly to the passive solar gain.

# *case study*   *The rock house, Menorca*

▼ **The planted roof terrace and stone steps provide a natural colour scheme.**

This house is located on the northern coast of Menorca, in an area of great natural beauty. The architect, Javier Barba of Barcelona, aimed to make the building as invisible as possible, integrating it into its rocky site.

It originally consisted of a derelict bungalow, garage and tower. To enlarge the living space, an excavation was made of the surrounding rock; the resulting sandstone was used in the new construction, to create the exterior walls. A new living area was opened up, the roof of which serves as a terrace. The tower was renovated to form a studio.

Local materials are used throughout, and much of the furniture is built in to ensure easy maintenance. The thick rock walls ensure that the building is cool during the summer.

The succulent plants on the roof are able to survive the hot summers and salty winds, and blend in with the plant cover in the surrounding area.

◄ Rough sandstone walls ensure that the house fits unobtrusively into the rocky cliff face.

◄ From above, the house is almost completely concealed within the slope of the rock.

# 4    Product design

The traditional definition of a well designed product is one that performs its function successfully; is manufactured efficiently, using appropriate materials and techniques; is easy to use; is safe; offers good value for money, and looks attractive. The relative importance of these criteria will vary from product to product. New definitions of good product design will include an environmental consideration: is the product designed to minimise the impact it has on the environment, during the whole of its life cycle?

➤ Commissioned by the manufacturers Junghans from the design consultancy FrogDesign in Germany, this clock uses 58 solar cells as an energy source. It produces 4,000 times more energy than the quartz movement consumes, the surplus energy being kept as a store for when light is unavailable. A radio link maintains the clock's accuracy, so that it does not need manual adjustment.

Designers can make a significant difference to the effect of a product because they are responsible for influencing the key decisions. These determine the choice of materials; how long the product will last; how effectively it uses energy, and how easily it may be reclaimed and re-used. The aims of the environment-conscious designer are to use the minimum resources throughout, to get the maximum possible use and value out of the least quantity of materials or energy, and to minimise pollution created during the manufacture and life of the product.

The pursuit of these objectives may clash with other demands: making a product quieter or cleaner may result in its being heavier or less efficient. Minimising the weight of materials involved may make the product less easy to recycle. The designer has to balance these competing demands, and ensure that the product is both saleable and also environmentally acceptable.

Much effort will be devoted to improving the environment performance of existing products. As part of an evolutionary process, products will be adapted, new materials used, energy efficiency improved, harmful side-effects minimised. In the longer term, however, there is plenty of scope for designers to look for a more revolutionary approach, where the conventional way of approaching a particular user need is challenged, and entirely new solutions emerge.

## Product life

Many products which used to be designed to last for years are now intended to have only a short lifespan. Disposability has been presented as a consumer benefit. Disposable lighters, pens, even watches, have been made possible by advanced technology reducing manufacturing costs, and there is often little incentive for the consumer to look after a product to ensure that it lasts, as it can so easily be replaced. Product life may be limited by changes in technology which make it obsolescent; by parts of the product simply wearing out through use, or by changes in fashion or style which make it old-fashioned and unattractive. Extending the life of a product is an obvious way of reducing waste. There are many different ways of achieving this, from improving reliability and durability so that it lasts longer, to making it recyclable so that the materials used to create it can have an additional life in another form.

### Extending useful life

The desire to reduce costs to make items such as kitchen appliances available to the mass market has led in many cases to products which are not robust enough to survive high usage. Often, different parts of the product deteriorate at different rates, but it is difficult to obtain and fit replacement parts, with the result that the entire product has to be discarded.

> Designed for easy disposal at the end of their life, these pens are manufactured from cardboard by Jet Pen of Berlin and Paris. They won a prize for their Polish designers, Ludowic, Orzelski and Nawrot, at the Design Forum Environmental Competition in Germany in 1989. The packaging consists of a single sheet of cardboard folded to construct a minimal box.

One way of extending a product's life is therefore simply to design it so that it can easily be maintained and serviced, by making those parts which are more susceptible to failure accessible and replaceable, and ensuring that the product is easy to disassemble and reassemble. With advanced products, repairs and replacements tend to have to be carried out by specialists, which means that product servicing becomes an important part of the total product offer. Agfa Gevaert have developed a photocopier designed to last for about ten years - twice as long as most copiers - and all repairs are carried out by Agfa as part of the hire arrangements.

Durability can also be achieved through the use of different technologies. New energy-efficient light bulbs last many times longer than traditional incandescent bulbs, for example.

### Design for re-manufacture

Product life may be extended simply by repairing small components over a period of time; however, if a product is difficult to service, or where several components may need replacement, the solution may lie in "re-manufacturing". This means that the product is disassembled, refurbished and re-assembled, incorporating new parts - or parts in better condition retrieved from other machines. The same approach can also be used where the product is technically functioning well, but the exterior appearance has deteriorated badly, or where major changes in colour requirements or surface finishes have rendered the product unfashionable. Major improvements in technology may also be incorporated into the product through re-manufacturing. The introduction of a more intelligent microprocessor system, which makes a domestic appliance more energy-efficient, may make it worthwhile to have the machine "up-graded", especially if its mechanical components are in good working order.

The restoration of used items is widely used in Third World countries where there is a shortage of indigenous manufacturing facilities, and where the labour costs involved in repair and re-manufacture are low relative to the cost of the materials involved. Products designed in the first place for eventual disassembly and re-manufacture need not involve high labour costs, however, although frequent design changes may inhibit re-manufacturing due to the difficulty associated with parts which are not interchangeable.

One of the dilemmas in designing for long life is the possibility that advances in materials or technology will make it possible to produce a new product which gives a greatly superior environment performance. Replacement of existing products may be a very desirable objective, but could result in considerable waste of resources unless the materials used can be recycled or adapted.

### Design for recyclability

Products eventually wear out or become obsolete. A high proportion of the cost of most manufactured goods is the cost of the raw materials, many of which are made from non-renewable resources; however, difficulties in retrieving and re-using these materials have often led to disposal in landfill sites. The cost of collection, transport, separation and recycling may well exceed the monetary - and even the environmental - cost of disposal. But with disposal costs steadily increasing and a growing demand from governments and consumers for the creation of systems to facilitate recycling, pressures are likely to

◄ Designed by the UK group Pentagram for Wilkinson Sword, the "Kompakt" razor uses a cassette system for carrying spare blades in the handle, which gives the razor its unusual shape. Made from metal, with a textured rubber grip, it is intended to combine durability with the convenience usually associated with a disposable item.

◄ The Japanese industrial designer Toshiyuki Kita and the American artist Keith Haring joined forces to design this stone and glass lamp with electroluminescent panels. Energy consumption is minimal, and the panels have a life of 10,000 hours. This is a rare example of the use of electroluminescence in domestic design; it is usually confined to industry.

➤ French designer
Thierry Kazazian, a
member of the O2
design group, created
this lamp, "Mazurka",
from used household
objects - a steamer,
whose overlapping
segments can be used
to change the intensity
of the light, and a
coffee filter that houses
a low-energy halogen
bulb.

increase substantially in support of design-ing with eventual recycling in mind.

Recycling can be more viable for large items, which can easily be collected and where the quantities of materials involved are significant. Ease of mechanical disas-sembly is important, with a minimum combination of different materials requir-ing separation. Zanussi's Nexus range of washing machines and dishwashers have a structure which is based on five modular sub-assemblies. A high proportion of the structure is moulded out of carboran, a recyclable advanced polymer which is also used to construct many of the functional components. The machines consist of fewer individual parts than usual, and additions like modular wiring and snap-on fixings make it easy to dismantle them for repair or recycling.

The reduction in the number of differ-ent materials used, and the use of single rather than composite materials, helps avoid the problem of material contamina-tion. Recycled materials which are made from a mixture of different substances - particularly mixtures of different poly-mers - have unpredictable behaviour char-acteristics, and can therefore be used only in restricted applications. In the longer term, it may be possible to develop highly sophisticated separation techniques through incorporating built-in tracers within the material, which might mean that guidelines for recyclability can be less restrictive.

Ideally, toxic materials should be replaced with non-hazardous alternatives; if this is not possible, they should be designed for easy identification and removal before the rest of the product is recycled. Batteries, for example, must be clearly identified so that they can be removed and safely disposed of before the product is recycled.

The sheer complexity of some prod-ucts, however, precludes reclamation, as discarded products may contain only very small quantities of recoverable materials. This is apparent in the miniaturisation of electronic products, where tiny quantities of valuable materials are incorporated within a case composed of several differ-ent, hard-to-recover, low-value materials. Miniaturisation has the advantage of reducing the quantities of materials needed in the first place, but it can make recycling impossible. It is unrealistic to believe that every product can be recycled, but this could prove an important part of

the life cycle of large items such as cars, domestic appliances, furniture and industrial equipment.

### Imposed lifetime

Designers have been accused of fuelling thoughtless consumerism by building in obsolescence, and encouraging replacement rather than repair, and disposal rather than re-use. "Newness" has been promoted as having an intrinsic value, and this has often been supported by real improvements in technology which make it possible to move to higher and higher levels of performance, as seen in the progression, for example, from tape cassette to compact disc to digital audio tape.

Increasing consumer demand for quality, and concern about waste, may result in a favouring of "classic" design approaches which do not date. Owning a product which is several years old may become a desirable self-statement, not something to be ashamed of because it indicates that the owner cannot afford to replace it.

However, advances in technology will continue, perhaps now fuelled by the need to improve environment performance. The introduction of CFC-free fridges will no doubt stimulate the replacement of existing fridges before they have reached the end of their useful life.

## Material selection

The material used has a major impact on the environment performance of a product, influencing its energy efficiency in manufacture and use, how easily it can be recycled, or whether it represents a hazard when eventually disposed of. There has been a huge growth in the number of materials available, with complex materials now specifically tailor-made for particular purposes.

Consideration of materials should begin at the earliest stage of the design process, with selection made in the context of how the product will be used, whether recycling is feasible, and what performance characteristics are demanded. A variety of different solutions may be appropriate.

### Quality specification

The over-specification of performance criteria may result in a heavier or higher-grade material being used than is necessary to meet the true functional

▲ Dorian Kurz, then a student at the Academy of Arts in Stuttgart, Germany, designed this larder to provide cooling and protection properties to rival those of the refrigerator. The free-standing aluminium-framed larder has three sections. The top section, shown here, uses terracotta to keep food cool. Water in an enamelled tray in the bottom of the section evaporates due to the flow of air through the ventilation slots: absorption and evaporation of the water by the porous clay keeps the unit cool. The ripple detailing increases the available surface area of the terracotta.

requirements of the product. Without, of course, sacrificing safety criteria, the designer should aim to use a material which is appropriate for the way in which the product will be used. Sometimes high-quality materials are specified because of their attractive appearance, but innovative design can create unusual and appealing images through the use of low-grade material which may be more appropriate to the product life cycle.

Against this must be set the danger that lower-quality materials will simply encourage disposability . One Japanese company, Papyrus, has produced a clock made out of corrugated cardboard (illustrations below). Does this encourage the clock to be disposed of after a short period of time, or will the durability of corrugated board give a result that lasts a realistic amount of time, after which the materials can be recycled or can biodegrade?

### Use of recycled materials

Some materials, such as glass and aluminium, offer almost identical performance and appearance characteristics after recycling, and are therefore already used extensively in recycled form as a standard raw material. Others, however, deteriorate or simply change in chemical composition during recycling, making them difficult to use again for their original purposes.

This is true particularly if different types of plastic are recycled together, as may be inevitable with reclamation from household waste. The resultant material is unlike any virgin material, but may have interesting properties in its own right. Increasingly, designers will be faced with the challenge of finding significant uses for recycled plastics. O2, a group of European designers, have produced a range of experimental products from fragmented, pressed plastic obtained from a collection of bottles, plastic bags, old toys and packaging materials. Pure recycled material, for example from PET bottles, is likely to become a mainstream ingredient of packaging material, just as recycled paper is.

Designers should always consider whether a recycled material might perform the function just as well as a virgin material, and should request a good selection of recycled materials from suppliers.

There is a "cascade" effect in the recycling of plastics: high-performance plastics, after recycling, cannot be used for their original application. After several passages through the recycling "loop", applications will be limited to very basic products, such as park benches or fence posts. This means that uses have to be found for recycled plastics in order to stimulate the development of a recycling infrastructure.

### Use of recyclable materials

There is little point in selecting a material which can be recycled if no mechanism exists, or is likely to exist, to enable it to be

recycled, or if the product has not been designed with easy recycling in mind.

Materials which are difficult to recycle may have other benefits, such as greater energy efficiency. The replacement in the automotive industry of easily recyclable steel and iron by hard-to-recycle plastics helped improve fuel consumption because of the savings that could be achieved in the weight of the car. However, the inclusion of higher quantities of plastic made it more difficult for scrap merchants to retrieve the metal parts, thus increasing their costs and diminishing the value of the metals recycling process. Efforts now being made to develop plastic components which are easy to dismantle and separate, and which be recycled themselves, may reduce this problem.

## Advanced materials

Much of the effort in materials development recently has been towards the creation of new materials which have unique properties, made through the integration of chemically different substances. To counteract the substitution of metals by plastic composites, metal producers have laminated or coated metals with plastic - making metal more difficult to recycle. Composite plastic materials have been developed to combine high strength with clarity, or heat resistance with flexibility. With ever-increasing numbers of new materials being produced, monitoring their environmental impact becomes

▼ Finding applications for low-grade recycled plastic material was the objective of a project undertaken for Montedison by designers Clare Brass and Silvio Caputo of O2 Design. These rubbish bins are part of a range covering street and domestic use.

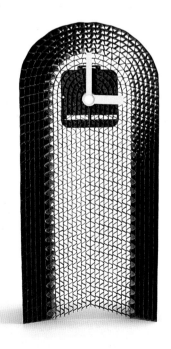

◄ ◄ "S Clock 1" (left) and "O Clock" (far left), from a series of elegant and attractive clocks made principally from corrugated card, designed by Eiji Hiyama of Papyrus in Tokyo. Does the use of this material encourage the clock to be disposed of after a short period of time, or will the card be durable enough to give a realistic life, after which the material can be recycled?

▼ Designed by Fiona Sharp and made in a small craft workshop in the UK, the "Acrobat" clothes drier/valet keeps both cost and conservation in mind. Made out of ash, a sustainably produced English hardwood, it achieves strength and stability out of the minimum amount of wood. Standing 1.45 metres high, it folds flat when not in use. Small details at the top and base are stained a deep indigo. It is designed for a long life, which justifies the quality of the materials and the time taken to manufacture it. The designer considers that small-scale workshops are better able to respond to the defects that occur in natural materials, and thus ensure less material wastage than would be likely with a large manufacturer.

almost impossible. However, the efforts being made to produce complex materials may also result in a greater understanding of how the materials can be separated out into their component parts for recycling.

Some advanced materials can give clear environmental benefits. Ceramics, such as silicon carbide and silicon nitrate, when mixed with aluminium, provide good solutions in applications where high temperature resistance enhances energy efficiency and therefore energy conservation. Super-strong, fine fibres made of graphite can be used as a construction material because they combine strength with light weight; they also produce less waste in manufacture than some of the alternatives. Advanced plastics can be valuable in medical applications, because they do not corrode like metal.

There is a tendency, however, for new materials to be developed simply in order to be different. A new material can be highlighted in the design of a car as an attractive "hi-tech" feature, when in fact the material offers no real improvement in performance. Unnecessary proliferation of material types - particularly of advanced composites - is not something the environment-conscious designer should encourage.

### Biodegradable materials

Many materials which were thought to be easily biodegradable have proved not to be when buried in landfill sites; even organic materials such as paper may take a long time to decompose. But natural substances such as wood and cotton are inherently biodegradable, and may therefore be preferable in many applications to plastics, which will not biodegrade.

The development of truly biodegradable plastics (see Chapter 5, "Packaging Design") may be useful for items which have to be disposed of after limited use, such as small components of surgical equipment. They might also be used for products which are regarded by consumers as disposable, especially for those which end up in the sewage system - although a better alternative might be to encourage re-usable products instead.

### Avoidance of hazardous ingredients

Designers should not specify any substance without first considering whether it has any dangers in use, such as a possible health risk, or whether it could create dangers in disposal. The use of polyurethane foam in soft furnishings is risky because of the toxic smoke produced when it burns; formaldehyde, often used in chipboard furniture, may be carcinogenic; heavy metals in paint can lead to problems if these are leached out into groundwater in landfill sites. The use of CFCs as the cooling medium in refrigerators and air-conditioning units will have to be phased out as alternatives are developed, and the same is true of CFCs used in the manufacturing of electronic components.

The Swedish automotive manufacturers Volvo aim to avoid the use of harmful substances as far as possible in all their vehicle production. Their objective is to eliminate completely the use of asbestos and mercury, for example.

Sometimes the hazardous substances are associated with secondary materials, such as paints and adhesives. Solvent-based paints should be replaced with water-based wherever possible, because solvents contribute to atmospheric pollution as well as polluting the working environment.

It is not always possible to identify easily the harmful side-effects of products - especially when these occur at the disposal stage of the product's life, rather than in use. It is important to ensure that the composition of materials is known fully, so that checks can be conducted on safety.

## Minimum use of material

A reduction in the amount of material used is desirable because of cost savings, in addition to the environment benefits of saving resources. A variety of approaches can be used.

*Simplification*
It is often the case that the simpler the design the less material it needs - provided that there is no hidden waste in the way materials are cut. Simplification may be achieved by clever component design, by the avoidance of purely decorative features or by making structures lighter in weight.

*Miniaturisation*
The reduction in size of electronic components has allowed items such as computers, televisions and calculators to be reduced in size, using smaller quantities of resources. As product shapes in many fields are no longer dictated by their mechanical components, new opportunities will emerge for the design form. Miniaturisation, however, tends to make it more difficult to reclaim the smaller quantities of material.

*Multi-functionalism*
One approach to minimising overall resource use is to develop products which

can perform a number of different functions, making proliferation unnecessary. Many kitchen appliances now combine at least two functions within one casing. The danger with this approach is that the multi-purpose object may perform each function slightly less well, or may perform a large number of trivial or even unnecessary functions. But the concept of the versatile, intelligent, multi-functional product must be an attractive one, and it offers major opportunities to the designer.

## Use of energy and water

One of the main contributions designers can make to improving the environment performance of products is in the area of energy use. They can design products which use energy efficiently, and which use as little energy as possible, and they can explore opportunities to use energy from renewable resources. Conservation of water supplies is also increasingly important, so opportunities to reduce water wastage should be sought.

### Energy efficiency
Legislation requiring appliances to be labelled with their energy consumption is stimulating the design of more efficient products in markets in the USA. Significant savings can be achieved - sometimes by extremely simple design changes. Designers at AEG in Germany have developed an oven which saves energy by the use of a removable divider so that only part of the oven needs to be heated up at a time. The build-up of ice on refrigerator and freezer walls causes the use of exces-

▲ This prototype water purifier, designed by Yorick Benjamin working with General Ecology Ltd in the UK, also functions as a kettle. Its sophisticated filtration system avoids the problem of toxins collecting in the filter, while a microchip sensitive to chlorine levels in the water indicates when the filter should be changed. A thick film heater - a printed element on a steel and ceramic insulator - gives better conductivity and therefore a more efficient boil rate than conventional heating elements. The product is manufactured with durability and recycling in mind: the internal electronics are all accessible for replacement, and no welding or adhesives have been used, so that components can be separated for metal recycling.

sive energy; Zanussi has created a moisture-free environment in the freezer by driving air through the compartment with a fan, which prevents the build-up of ice.

Sometimes, energy wastage may go completely unnoticed. Televisions with remote control devices and "instant on" standby features consume electricity even when they are not being used.

The incorporation of microprocessors into domestic appliances can help save energy. A tumble drier which can detect how much water is left on clothes can choose the correct setting in order to minimise the amount of electricity used. Timing controls allow appliances to be used during the night, when energy needs can be supplied more easily.

Energy efficiency is important during the manufacturing stage, too. Many materials are highly energy-intensive in production - aluminium, for example - but that energy cost may be justified by energy savings delivered in use, and by length of life through recycling.

It has been suggested that considerable energy savings, as well as cost savings, can be achieved by allowing the end user of a product to assemble it. Assembling and transporting goods such as furniture and domestic appliances are costly; producing simple and easily assembled components would reduce manufacturing and transport costs.

### Alternative energy sources

The contribution made to national power supplies by renewable forms of energy such as solar, tidal and wind power is likely to increase steadily in many countries. For most powered products, mains electricity or gas is likely to be the most practical source of energy, but there may be opportunities to use solar or wind power directly. The solar-powered calculator is an example of an everyday item with low power requirements, for which light is a very efficient and convenient source of power. Solar power is particularly valuable in areas where no other form of energy is readily available.

Batteries offer a convenient but very inefficient way of storing energy. Mains power should be used wherever possible. Recent developments making batteries renewable help to minimise the problems caused by battery disposal, but do little to improve overall energy efficiency.

### Water use

Mechanical changes to products can reduce the amount of water they use. By increasing mechanical pressure, and ensuring that water is directed to where it is needed, it has been possible to develop a washing machine which uses significantly less water.

The redesign of the toilet cistern can also reduce water consumption, as in a new design from Swedish manufacturer Ifö Sanitär (see pages 82-3).

## Minimising pollution

Air, water and noise pollution can be reduced and prevented by designers carefully considering the selection of product materials, and by looking for alternatives to conventional approaches.

The automobile is one of the worst polluters. One way of addressing this problem is to try to produce cleaner cars by using power from electricity, methane or other cleaner fuel sources and by developing new types of engine, such as the lean-burn, which use sophisticated electronics and modified cylinder heads for a fuller combustion and a destruction of the potential air pollutants. A more fundamental solution is to develop efficient alternatives to car usage, in the form of public transport systems. This is increasingly winning approval in major cities, where the use of cars causes major problems of congestion and noise in addition to pollution.

Noise is a form of pollution which is often overlooked, but which causes discomfort and irritation. Many kitchens are used as living areas for the family, and the noise generated by appliances is continuously tackled by designers. New materials can virtually eliminate the internal resonance within the appliance cabinet, through their vibration-absorption properties. Mechanical devices, such as pneumatic dampers fitted in suspension units, and insulated suspension springs, can further minimise noise transmission.

### Reducing the impact of pollution

Although the ideal is to prevent the risk of pollution in the first place, there are still many areas where pollution has to be addressed after it has occurred. The catalytic converter chemically cleans up car exhaust emissions once they have been produced, converting fumes into water vapour and less harmful emissions. Such "end of pipe" approaches to reducing manufacturing pollution have been criticised by environmentalists as only a partial solution. In the short term, though, designers and engineers will be asked to develop more effective ways of controlling emissions, and better ways of disposing of waste materials, through finding new uses for them.

## The impact of new technology

New technologies can make more effective use of resources. The development in the telecommunications industry of fibre optics, made from glass, a renewable resource, will reduce demand for copper, of which there are only limited supplies. Fibre optic systems should be safer, more effective and less costly in terms of resource consumption.

The microwave oven uses far less energy than a conventional oven; intelligent home-management systems can ensure that heating systems are used efficiently, and sophisticated electrical spraying devices can mean that very small amounts of pesticides can be used to cover large areas of crops, as the product is dispersed accurately and evenly.

Of course, any new technology brings with it some uncertainty, because the long-term consequences of its use are unknown. However, it seems clear that the incorporation of appropriate advanced technology into products and processes can make a significant contribution to improving their environment performance. It is up to the designer to be well informed about the possibilities of new developments.

▲ Increased interest in the bicycle as a convenient and unpolluting form of transport may stimulate innovation in design and material use. The Velo-4, designed by Michael Conrad and Dieter Raefler in Germany, has a self-supporting fibre compound frame, which is not subject to the corrosion that affects steel frames. The Velo-4 is also extremely stable, in spite of a low weight.

# *case study* *Dolphin-Wilding furniture, UK*

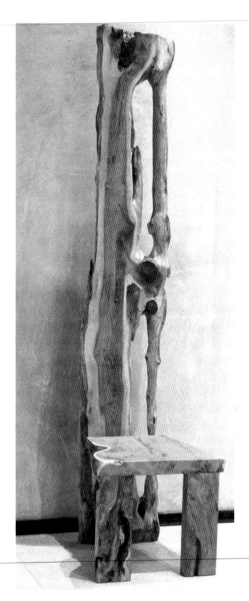

Driftwood, waste wood from demolished buildings and nautical paraphernalia are the materials that London-based Julienne Dolphin-Wilding uses to make her unusual one-off pieces of furniture. Huge, graceful, high-backed chairs are functional for indoor or outdoor use, and create unusual and witty decorative pieces. Non-toxic wood treatments and natural finishes such as beeswax and salt scrubbing are used to allow the wood to breathe.

All the materials used would otherwise be left for waste. They take on a new role which exploits their individuality and irregularity - precisely those characteristics which preclude their use in most applications. Decoration is achieved through the use of knotted ropes and metal fittings. The inherent qualities and features of the primitive materials used inspire the themes for the designs.

▲ ➤ These items of furniture can take on epic proportions, becoming a striking feature in any room. Chairs become objects of interest and play value, attractive scupltures which are also functional.

▲ Detail of the roped
back of a chair.

# *case study*  *Ifö Acqua toilet, Scandinavia*

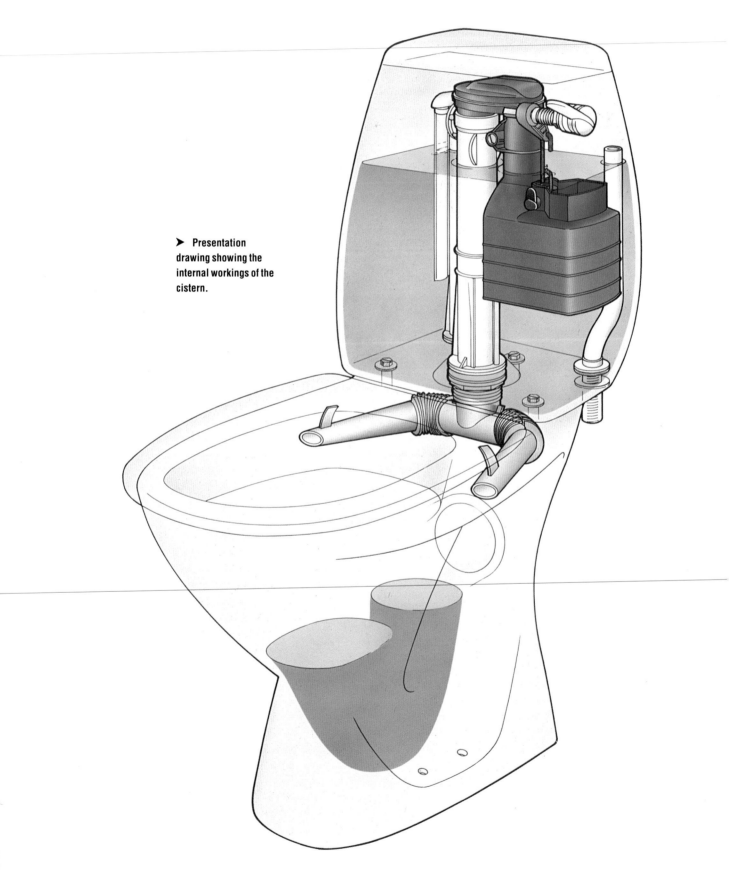

➤ Presentation drawing showing the internal workings of the cistern.

About 30 per cent of the water consumed by a household is used to flush the toilet - an obvious waste of processed, drinkable water. Ifö Sanitär of Sweden set out to develop a toilet which could operate with a much lower quantity of water, aiming to save over a third of the water used by traditional products.

Merely reducing the amount of water flushed from the cistern, however, was not the answer. The entire product had to be considered to ensure that it was effective. The design of the bowl and rim, the rate of the flow of water, the performance of the gravity drainage system - all had to be thought through to develop an integrated solution. The six-litre single flush system was achieved by the use of a special twin diverter flush tube which ensures efficient, effective use of a reduced quantity of water.

The redesign of the mechanics of the product was accompanied by an attempt to produce a more attractive sculptural form, which would have a classic, long-lasting appeal. Knud Holscher Industrial Design of Denmark developed an elegant, durable shape to meet this need. The product has also been designed for easy maintenance; repairs can be carried out without the need to dismantle the cistern or any major components. The compact, free-standing design gives flexibility to bathroom layouts, helping the efficient use of space.

◄ The innovative interior mechanical design of the Ifö Acqua was accompanied by exterior styling which positions the product as an attractive, contemporary object. It was important, however, for the product not to look out of place in a conventional bathroom.

# *case study*   *AEG, Germany*

Reducing the amount of electricity used in washing machines, often the commonest and most used household appliances, can make a significant contribution to energy conservation. The German company AEG, which consistently aim to improve the environment impact of their products, have developed the new Lavamat to achieve low energy and water consumption through a sophisticated microprocessor and sensor system.

The build-up of soap suds in the machine is monitored, and excess suds are avoided throughout the wash by partially reducing the spin speed. Because the level of suds is controlled, less water is required to rinse the clothes.

A load sensor automatically relates the amount of water required to the type and size of load, again ensuring that only the minimum amount of water and energy is used. This is particularly important when the machine is not loaded to its full capacity, although the manufacturers encourage users to fill machines whenever possible.

The wide range of programmes include energy-saving wash programmes, and a low-temperature wash for cotton fabrics. The incorporation of a microprocessor allows great flexibility and

◀ The Lavamat's conventional exterior conceals a wide range of intelligent features which improve environment performance, while not affecting washing quality.

▼ AEG's advertising campaign in the UK is clearly targetted at the "green consumer". The functional performance of the product is taken for granted, and the focus of interest is purely on its environment performance.

control to ensure that fabrics are well cared for.

The Lavamat minimises the amount of undissolved powder emitted, since the risk of water pollution is greater if the detergent is undissolved. The machine has a special valve in the sump which is automatically closed by water pressure from the expansion tank before a programme starts; on filling with water, no undissolved powder can be trapped in the drainage system. This effectively saves about 20 per cent of the washing powder normally recommended for use.

Reliability and long life are also important. An unevenly spread load can lead to increased wear to the drum and bearings when the machine spins. Sensors in the Lavamat detect an unbalanced load and redistribute it evenly. The outer surface, tub and stainless steel drive are all protected from corrosion. One additional benefit of the electronically controlled transmission system, and the amount of insulation, is that the machine is very quiet in operation.

These features of increased intelligence, lower energy consumption and better water economy will no doubt be the objectives of future product development in this sector.

# *case study* *Volvo concept car, Sweden*

> ➤ The concept car brings together many examples of current best practice in car design.

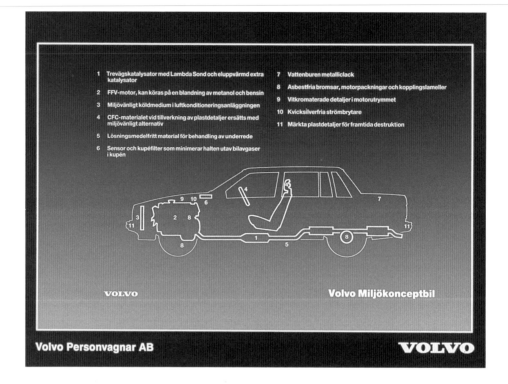

1  Trevägskatalysator med Lambda Sond och eluppvärmd extra katalysator
2  FFV-motor, kan köras på en blandning av metanol och bensin
3  Miljövänligt köldmedium i luftkonditioneringsanläggningen
4  CFC-materialet vid tillverkning av plastdetaljer ersätts med miljövänligt alternativ
5  Lösningsmedelfritt material för behandling av underrede
6  Sensor och kupéfilter som minimerar halten utav bilavgaser i kupén
7  Vattenburen metalliclack
8  Asbestfria bromsar, motorpackningar och kopplingslameller
9  Vitkromaterade detaljer i motorutrymmet
10  Kvicksilverfria strömbrytare
11  Märkta plastdetaljer för framtida destruktion

VOLVO          Volvo Miljökonceptbil

Volvo Personvagnar AB          VOLVO

▲ From its outside bodywork, the environmental concept car looks deceptively like any other car.

Volvo aims to reduce the environmental damage caused by cars through effective control measures in the manufacturing processes, and through the implementation of an environment policy which affects the entire life cycle of the car, from design to disposal. Considerable research has been devoted to reducing the weight of components, to improve fuel efficiency and reduce resource consumption. New materials such as carbon fibre have been considered.

Volvo's environmental concept car demonstrates what can be achieved with existing technology. The solutions presented in 1990 either already existed, or were shortly about to be available. The features demonstrated in the concept car include:

● An engine which runs on a mixture of methanol and petrol, cutting the release of carbon monoxide and hydrocarbons by half. The engine is to be developed further with the aim of meeting the requirements expected to be set in California by the turn of the century.

● A heated catalytic converter, which reduces exhaust emissions. During a normal drive, most emissions take place during the first two minutes, while the engine and catalytic converter are still cold. With the converter electrically heated, it becomes effective in only 30 seconds.

● The elimination of CFCs, including those in the air-

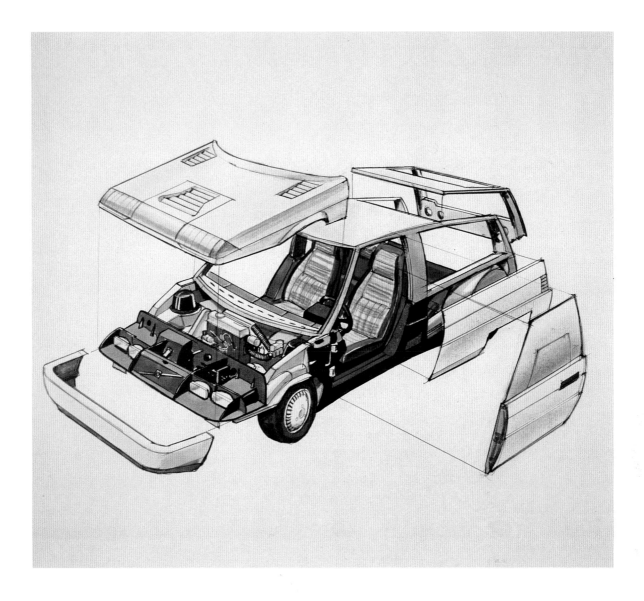

conditioning unit. By 1993, Volvo regard it as a realistic goal
to have phased out CFCs as foaming and mould-release
agents in the manufacture of polyurethane foam for parts
such as seat fillings and steering wheels.

● The use of waterborne metallic paint, which dramatically
reduces solvent discharges. A solvent-free underseal, known
as hot melt, means that hydrocarbon discharges can be
significantly reduced.

● The elimination of harmful substances such as asbestos and
mercury from brake linings and clutch plates.

● A filter to prevent exhaust fumes from being drawn into the
inside of the car.

● Identification of plastic parts, so that specific plastics can be
removed and recycled when the car is eventually disposed of.

Volvo have maintained a consistency of car styling which makes it
difficult sometimes to identify how old a car is. The classic design
is intended to have a timeless quality which is appropriate for
Volvo's claim to offer high quality, reliable cars which can last for
much longer than many other makes. The concept car therefore
maintains this classic style, rather than striving for an overtly
"futuristic" look.

▲ For many years,
Volvo have been
exploring lightweight
component cars, in
which the use of
materials such as
plastic and aluminium
can significantly
reduce fuel
consumption.

# case study General Motors electric car, USA

▲ The prototype electric Impact car on a test run. The styling shows that the makers intend the car to appeal to the top end of the market.

Automotive manufacturers have for years been investigating the use of battery power as an alternative to petrol. Many approaches have been based on the modification of cars powered by petrol or diesel. The Impact car, however, has been designed from the start to overcome some of the main shortcomings of electric vehicles, such as limited range and performance. Advances in electronics and electric motor design, lightweight structural materials and aerodynamic styling help contribute to the Impact's performance - a top speed of 100 mph, a range of 125 miles between charging, and acceleration from 0 to 60 mph in 8 seconds. The 32 lead acid batteries can be charged from the mains in four to five hours. Running efficiency is claimed to be about twice that of petrol-driven cars.

The use of electricity and batteries to power cars, although avoiding the direct pollution problems of petrol, does not create an environmentally perfect solution. The power to charge batteries is generated from highly polluting processes, and even rechargeable batteries represent relatively inefficient ways of storing power. However, there is no doubt that electrically powered vehicles are less polluting, even when power station emissions are taken into consideration. This makes them attractive in some urban situations, such as Los Angeles, California. It is anticipated that the number of electric cars and vans on the roads of Los Angeles could increase sharply as part of a comprehensive effort by the city to reduce smog problems.

One disadvantage of electric cars is the high cost of recycling or disposing of the batteries. However, new, longer-lasting, faster-charging batteries are being developed.

▼ Presentation
sketches and prototype
of the Impact car,
showing the interior
layout and the body
shell.

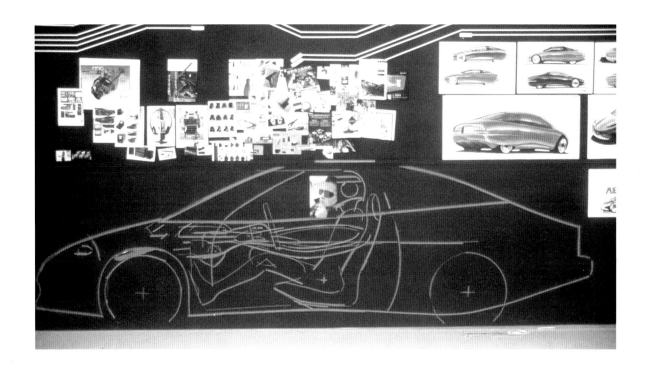

# 5    Packaging design

Packaging designers have demonstrated a great deal of ingenuity and inventiveness over the last few years, helping manufacturers deliver convenience and freshness to customers, and finding new ways to "add value" to the product through aesthetic or practical benefits. The way in which a product is packaged is often one of the major influences on whether people notice it and buy it, particularly in markets such as perfume and cosmetics where image plays a crucial role. The cost of packaging can be more than the cost of the product inside.

We are increasingly aware, however, of the impact that packaging has on the environment. Both the quantity of packaging, and the use of particular types of material, are being questioned. The visibility of packaging in the waste stream has prompted consumer concerns: it accounts for around one-third of household waste in most countries in Europe and North America, and is a clearly recognisable component of litter. As packaging materials become more sophisticated and elaborate, disposing of them after they have been used only once appears to be a waste of valuable resources. Producing and disposing of packaging can cause environment problems just like any other product: pollution in the manufacturing process; the consumption of energy and non-renewable resources, and the dangers of hazardous ingredients being dispersed into groundwater or the air during disposal through landfill or incineration.

Under the current structure of our manufacturing, distribution and retailing chain, and with current consumer expectations, packaging has a variety of roles. Its main function - to ensure that the product inside reaches the consumer in good condition - is often taken for granted, but it ensures that as little as possible of the product is wasted or damaged during distribution and storage. Packaging also delivers the benefits of hygiene and safety, which are increasingly important to consumers because of fears of contamination or tampering. It enables the product to be handled easily, stacked, stored and transported. And, of course, packaging helps consumers identify the product in the store - an important function in self-service stores with vast ranges of merchandise. Finally, it is a major communication vehicle, providing information and usage instructions.

Many environmentalists are calling into question the environmental cost of this type of production and distribution structure. They propose a return to more locally based economies, where the chain between producer and consumer is shorter, reducing the need for so much packaging. However, within the current structure, there are many ways of reducing the environment impact of packaging, often without compromising consumer and producer demands for functional performance and visual appeal.

In many countries, legislation will influence changes. The EC waste management strategy requires industry to minimise waste overall, with packaging identified as a specific area where there is room for improvement. Targets are proposed for the proportion of packaging which can be re-used or recycled, which will determine material choice in various sectors such as drinks containers. The hierarchy of "reduce, re-use, recycle" will underpin the EC approach.

The shortage of landfill sites in the US has stimulated a variety of local laws. These include deposits on soft drinks containers to encourage their return, and the requirement that householders separate out waste so that it can be recycled.

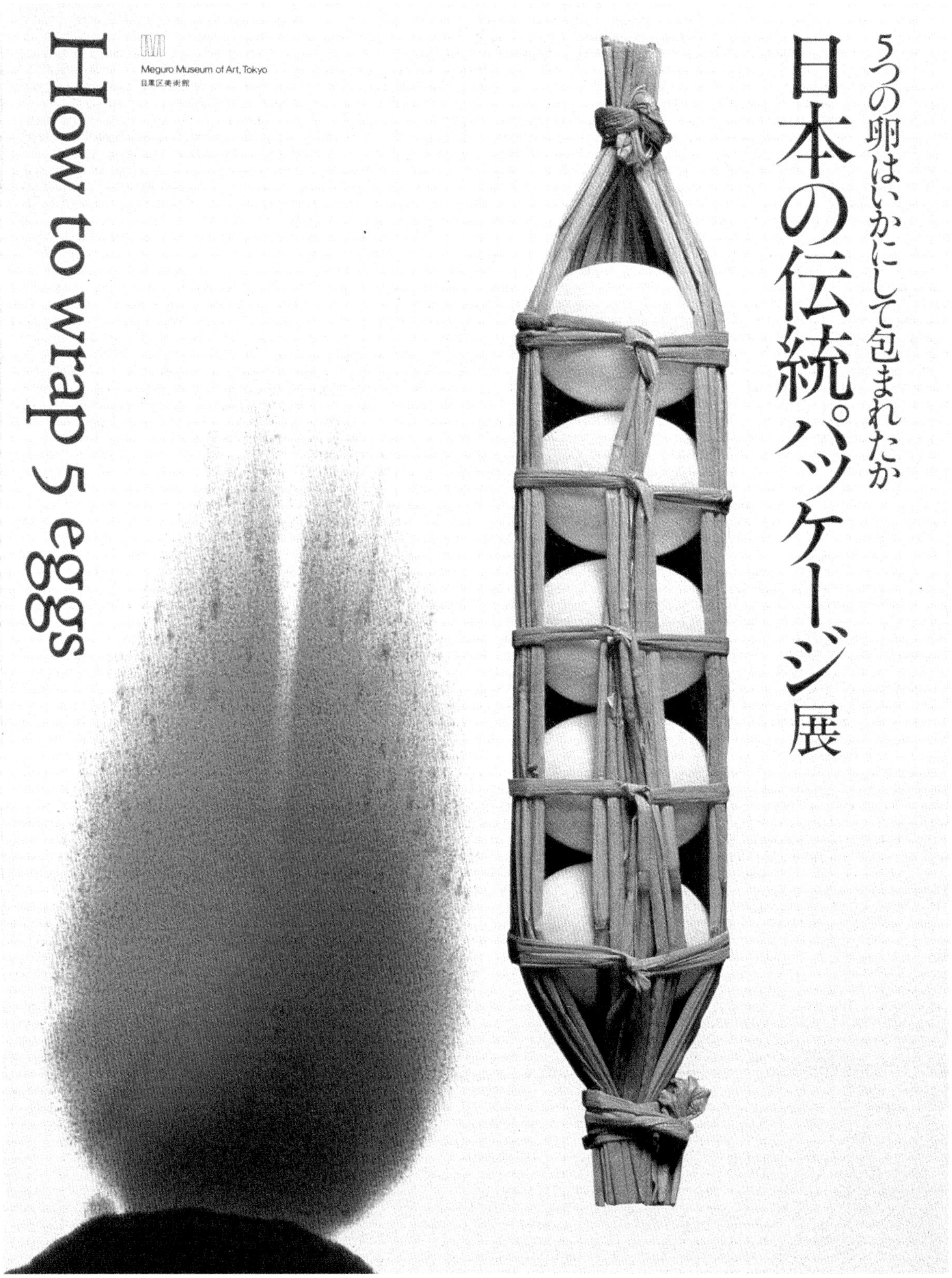

5つの卵はいかにして包まれたか
日本の伝統パッケージ展

How to wrap 5 eggs

Meguro Museum of Art, Tokyo
目黒区美術館

The combination of consumer concerns and legislative pressure will ensure that environment impact becomes an essential criterion in the design of packaging material. In this area, as in other design areas, new ways of working will be required, and new aesthetics will evolve. The challenge for designers is to produce packaging that sells the product, and protects it effectively, but creates less environment damage.

Designing packaging for minimum impact requires an understanding of the complete life of the pack, from the production of the material through to manufacture, distribution, end use and disposal. While the overall objective should be to use the minimum resources, the best solution depends largely on context. What type of product is it? How will it be used? Where will it be used? The designer will have to consider a complex range of options to identify the best solution.

The material used in packaging, the way the pack is constructed, and the way it is merchandised in the store will be particularly important considerations for the packaging designer. Graphic designers, who often take the lead in packaging design, will have to place more emphasis on technical issues related to production and to the properties of materials if they are to play a leading role in innovation to improve environment performance. Close collaboration between graphic designers, industrial designers, technologists and materials scientists will be important. Producers of packaging materials will find it essential to provide clear, objective information about the performance of their products, in areas like energy efficiency, recyclability and additives.

Products have very different packaging requirements. Delicate items of medical equipment have to be treated quite differently from shampoo, and washing machines differently from food, so generalisations about material usage and packaging construction are difficult to make. Improvements in environment impact can be made in a wide variety of ways - it is up to the designer to determine what may be appropriate, feasible and desirable for a particular product.

The selection of material may depend entirely on where the product will be used.

◄ ► Industrial ingredients are often distributed in dry granular form in steel drums, which can lead to high storage and transport costs. This alternative, made from corrugated board, was developed by Reed Corrugated Cases with Sams Design. The hinged plastic lid, incorporating an anti-tamper device, provides a waterproof seal. The square box gives better space use than a round steel drum, and the boxes can be stored flat before and after use, saving on storage space.

A refillable glass bottle designed for several re-uses may use less energy than a plastic bottle. However, if these bottles are miniatures, as used on airlines, their weight is important. Because glass is much heavier than plastic, using plastic results in a saving for the airline in terms of fuel consumed during flying. This energy saving therefore has to be set against the energy lost when the bottles are disposed of. It is clear, therefore, that the equations can be highly complex.

## Avoiding over-packaging

A frequent criticism of packaging is that more is used than is really needed to meet the requirements of functional performance. This is particularly true of luxury items such as confectionery and cosmetics, and of products packed in single-serve units or blister packs. Significant reductions in the amount of packaging used for some products may be achievable only with some trade-off in consumer convenience, or with changes in usage patterns, or in expectations about product appearance. There may be opportunities for

designers to adopt a radical departure from conventional norms. Packaging an expensive perfume, or selection of chocolates, in a box made from simple corrugated board may actually be interesting and attractive to consumers!

An elaborate and sophisticated pack may deliver a marginal benefit to the consumer, but simpler alternatives may be preferable from an environmental viewpoint. Aerosol packs are an example of over-packaging, where a small quantity of product is contained within a large pack. The performance characteristics of aerosols may make their use necessary in certain specialised applications - such as medicine - but they may no longer be considered appropriate for everyday uses when good alternative delivery systems exist. If aerosols could be easily recycled they might cause less environmental concern, but so far recycling appears to be difficult to achieve.

The ratio of product cost to packaging cost varies depending on whether the product is cheap but difficult to package, such as household or garden chemicals, or expensive but technically simple to

package, like butter. The designer therefore has to consider each application separately, to reduce material and energy usage without compromising the protection of the pack or its other important functions.

**Using minimum amounts of material**
Manufacturers have a strong cost incentive to reduce the amount of packaging materials used. Not only are raw material costs reduced with lighter or smaller packs, but distribution and storage costs are also saved. A re-design of the aluminium soft drinks can to reduce the diameter of the opening end allowed a reduction in the amount of material used per can. Removing the base cup of a bottle made of PET lightened it by nearly one third. However, lightweighting has to be considered in the context of the entire life cycle of the pack: creating a very light pack may not be desirable if it is possible to use the pack again, when strength would become important.

In packs which are "one-trip", or which go into the recycling system, reducing the quantity of materials is usually beneficial, because of savings in energy and in materials. The shape of a pack can have a significant impact on the amount of energy used in transportation. The use of a square-sectioned package rather than a circular pack gives a more efficient way of transporting products like milk, as more unit product can be contained in the allotted space. An octagonal corrugated box used by one home-delivery pizza chain uses 10 per cent less material than the usual square box, and also delivers a more appealing product because toppings no longer smudge on the pizza lid.

Reduction in the quantity of materials used may also be achieved by considering the packaging requirements in the context of merchandising and in-store dispensing opportunities. A protective outer display at point of sale may reduce the need for a layer of secondary packaging.

The creation of unusual bottle and cap shapes can use more material than necessary. A double-walled cap on a shampoo bottle uses more material than a small screw cap; a complex, novel shape tends to be less efficient than a standard cylindrical shape. The desire to create a novel appearance - to give extra impact or to reflect the image the product wishes to convey - may be at odds with materials minimisation. Striking graphics can add interest to simple, standard containers. It is possible, as consumers become more critical of the environment impact of packaging, that they will become more approving of simple, straightforward packaging structures, and less likely to place novelty and distinctiveness quite so high on their selection criteria.

◄ "Crazy Cosmetics",
designed for Swiss
company Modima by
Yellow Design,
Pforzheim, Germany.
Crazily shaped black
glass bottles, with
interchangeable
plastic tops, create
dramatic on-shelf
impact, as well as
amusing bathroom
"architecture",
depending on how they
are arranged. There is
no secondary
packaging for the
individual bottles, as
product information is
contained in a small
folded leaflet stuck to
the base. The whole set
is sold in a box made
from recycled foam.

In some sectors, additional layers of packaging have been introduced to protect the product from being tampered with. Incorporating a tamper-evident feature into a closing device may be an effective and less wasteful solution.

### Material quality

Another form of over-packaging is the specification of high-quality materials where functional performance and consumer taste do not require them - for example, the use of virgin white card in outer cartons.

Very often, material composition or weight is specified by habit, rather than by a real examination of the needs of the job. The increased use of recycled materials in the packaging industry can play a significant part in reducing overall resource consumption, and thus every effort should be made to specify these where their use is acceptable in terms of functional performance and aesthetic appeal.

## Re-use and refill

Resource conservation may take the form of the re-use or refilling of containers, thus extending their functional lifetime. After minimising the use of resources in the first place, this route appears most environmentally attractive. However, the process of re-using and refilling has an environ-

mental cost too, which must be considered. The energy cost of collecting and cleaning containers should not outweigh the energy value of manufacturing them in the first place, and packs may have to be re-used many times before the initial investment in energy is recouped, so durability will be important. Containers also have to be designed so that they can be cleaned easily.

There are a variety of ways in which a refillable system can work. The container can be returned to the manufacturer for refilling; the user can take the container to a refilling point; or the user can purchase a refill pack from which a more durable container can be refilled. Whether any of these approaches is appropriate and beneficial will depend on the manufacturing and distribution systems involved and, of course, on the nature of the product itself.

### Returnable, refillable systems

Return systems that operate in a closed loop between manufacturer and user have traditionally been widely used in the beverage industry. In the UK, doorstep milk delivery depends on consumers returning empty bottles quickly. In the food service trade, bottles and casks are returned to the manufacturer and many food items, such as bread, are supplied in re-usable crates. Where it is possible for the delivery system to double up as the collection system, with outlets relatively close to the manufacturer or distribution centre, this system can be highly efficient. Difficulties arise, however, if products are internationally traded; then, return systems work only if there is standardisation of packs, with every manufacturer participating in the re-use process.

While the collection of packs for re-use can be relatively easy if large numbers of packs accumulate at one point, as in a restaurant, it becomes more difficult for products consumed at home. Increasingly, however, retailers are accepting returned containers - particularly glass bottles - and in some countries this is becoming the normal system as bottle deposits are introduced via the retailer.

### Consumer refill points

Many years ago, shoppers would take along their own containers to be filled directly in the shop from sacks or casks of product. In France and other countries, table wine is still sold in this way. This approach can be highly attractive in terms of environment considerations, particularly as there are savings in energy cost by avoiding the "return" route. Although

➤ A self-dispensing milk refill machine, used throughout the Tengelmann supermarket chain in Germany since 1988. Glass and recyclable plastic bottles containing one litre are purchased at the store and filled with milk at the machine. When emptied, they are cleaned and brought back for refilling by the customer without limit to the number of times they can be used. In Munich alone, the system resulted in the saving of 3,700 tonnes of packaging waste in one year.

containers need to be durable, they do not need to be able to survive numerous circuits through the distribution system.

The original container may be purchased with the first purchase of the product and replaced when necessary, or a variety of alternative containers might be offered separately, allowing the consumer to choose whatever is the most convenient size, shape, etc. The only important criterion is that the container should be able to protect the product effectively and should be easy to clean.

Consumers obviously have to be willing to accept a trade-off in terms of convenience, although the refilling process could be offered as an intrinsic part of the attraction of the product. In the case of the UK-based franchise The Body Shop, for example, refills are offered at a discounted price compared with the original packaged product.

**Refill packs**
In the short term, refill packs may offer the most practical way of achieving re-use in many categories. One durable container, appropriate for storing the product and using it, is sold. Additional product requirements are supplied via refill packs, which need have only a short life expectancy, and can therefore be made from a small quantity of lighter-weight or lower-quality material. The refill pack can also be easier and less heavy for the consumer to take home. Soft-sided, collapsible refill packs take up considerably less room in landfill sites.

With detergents, shampoos and other household products which are in very regular use, refill sachets or cartridges could allow the original pack to be more attractively and more intelligently designed, because the extra cost of this will be spread across a much longer life, and packaging costs overall are reduced by avoiding the need to throw away significant quantities of material.

Refill packs must be easy and clean to use, rather than messy and inconvenient. Pouring spouts and easy-to-tear openings can be helpful.

## Material choice

There is considerable confusion about whether some materials are inherently less damaging to the environment than others. Some may consume more energy or non-renewable materials in their production, but perhaps have a longer life span. Some are easier to recycle, while others are believed to degrade easily and harmlessly. When disposed of by incineration, some materials are valuable because their energy content can be reclaimed, but there may be concerns about the substances released into the atmosphere during the incineration process. No one type of material can claim overall environmental superiority. Material selection has to be considered, therefore, as part of the total manufacturing and design process, taking into account the entire life cycle of the product and pack.

### Use of recyclable material

Packaging uses valuable materials which could be reclaimed and re-used rather than dumped in landfill sites. The contribution made by the use of recyclable materials depends entirely on whether there is an end use for the materials once reclaimed. Glass may be recycled and re-used to make containers that are indistinguishable from the originals. Other materials, however, such as plastic, are more difficult to recycle, and the recycled substances may have very different properties and appearances from the original, making them unsuitable for re-use for the same purpose. Recycled materials have to have a market, and this depends on a variety of factors, including the cost difference between recycled and virgin materials.

Most reclaimed materials come from industrial and commercial waste, where there are large quantities of identifiable materials which can be collected and processed efficiently. Most packaging ends up in household waste, with small quantities of different materials widely dispersed, posing a huge challenge for collection and sorting. Major efforts are being made to encourage the reclamation of household

▲ A table-top dispenser for liquid sweeteners, designed by Packaging Innovation for the Japanese market. A clear glass refill pack sits inside a moulded plastic bottle with a handle. Each press of the pump dispenses a measured amount of sweetener. Minimally designed refill packs which work with permanent dispensers will become increasingly common for domestic use. The use of glass in this case might be thought excessive because of its weight; a re-usable, recyclable plastic refill might be an improvement.

▲ Bales of crushed soft drinks containers made from PET are now collected and stored for recycling in many countries.

waste. Bottle and can banks are now common in many countries, and many local areas are experimenting with kerbside collection schemes. The high participation rates achieved demonstrate the public commitment to recycling, but there are still problems in sorting, grading and re-using many materials.

Designing for recyclability is worthwhile only where there is a recycling infrastructure, or where the manufacturer makes arrangements to collect the used packs. There also has to be an end use to which the recycled material can be put.

Recycling is assisted if composite materials or multiple layers of different materials are avoided. The use of one single material throughout avoids the problems of contamination and unpredictable performance which can arise from mixed materials.

Identification of the type of material can also be important in sorting. This may be done by consumers at home, or by a mechanical sorting process in a municipal waste site. Clear visual symbols will help consumers, while in the long term the incorporation of "tracers" within the material itself may allow selection and sorting to be carried out mechanically.

While collection and recycling systems are quite well established for glass and cans, plastic is far behind in most places, making it look relatively unattractive as a packaging material if glass is a realistic alternative. However, if plastic can be recycled, its high energy efficiency and other benefits change the picture significantly.

**Use of recycled material**

Packaging materials have used recycled ingredients for years. Cans are manufactured from material which contains a high proportion of secondary, reclaimed metal; outer packaging such as corrugated board uses waste-based pulp. The production of aluminium cans is made economic by using waste aluminium, as producing virgin aluminium has very high energy costs. The issue for designers now is whether more recycled materials can be used, as part of the process of stimulating demand and encouraging efficient recycling.

*Paper and card*

Recycled papers and cards are often adequate to meet the functional requirements of a pack, although the occurrence of contaminants prevents the use of recycled material directly in contact with food or healthcare products since there might be a possible health risk. Recycled paper has performance and appearance characteristics which are very different from those of virgin paper (see Chapter Six, "Printing and graphic design"). It can be used to great effect, however, even in the packaging of luxury items.

*Plastic*

Most plastics are not difficult to recycle if they can be isolated, but changes in chemical structure do occur, and the recycled product may perform unpredictably, making its use rather difficult in applications where precise characteristics are required. The products generally associated with

> Alberto's "Pure and Clear" range of hair care products are packed in PET bottles. The clarity of the packaging material is used to emphasise the "pure" nature of the product ingredients. PET is fully recyclable, provided the infrastucture exists to collect it.

◄ A premium range of pasta sauces, manufactured in the USA by International Gourmet Specialities, "Classico" is based on regional Italian recipes. The labels, designed by Duffy Design Group, are printed in four colours on Speckletone recycled paper, to give a rustic and traditional appearance. The glass jars are recyclable.

▼ "Bio Packs", produced by the Bio Pack company in Germany, are paper pouches filled with straw or other fibres. They give a flexible, absorbent, non-dusty packing material, which can be easily shaped around fragile objects. They are easy to re-use and clean to store, but if discarded they will decompose on a compost heap. They make a good alternative to polystyrene.

recycled plastic tend to be low-quality items such as builders' sheets, garbage bags and flower pots. However, there may be increasing opportunities to use recycled plastic in packaging materials. PET (polyethylene terephthalate), a clear, high-quality plastic often used for soft drinks containers, can be recycled. Material made from post-consumer PET waste has been used by Procter and Gamble in the packaging of household cleaning products. Designers should be open to the use of recycled materials of all kinds, where these materials can meet the essential performance requirements of the pack.

The cost of using recycled materials relative to virgin materials varies widely. Difficulties in obtaining high-quality waste, and the small scale of many recycling efforts, can make recycled materials expensive. In the longer term, however, the increased use of recycled material should lower packaging costs. In the meantime, it may be possible to justify the small additional cost because of consumer willingness to support recycling efforts: packaging which is perceived to be environmentally sensitive can deliver an "added value" benefit, and create differentiation among competitors.

### Biodegradable materials

Biodegradability has been proposed as one answer to the problem of the accumulation of ever-increasing quantities of long-lived materials such as plastics; it has also been suggested that biodegradable packaging could reduce the litter problem. But materials which biodegrade relatively easily - like paper - can give only limited protection to a product, and are therefore often coated with substances to make them resistant to decomposition. However, assumptions about the speed of degradation have recently been challenged, with the discovery in US landfill sites of almost perfectly preserved newspapers and even food: without exposure to air and water, biodegradability takes a very long time. Photodegradability - destruction through exposure to sunlight - has been explored as an option for plastic garbage bags, and for packaging which might end up as litter. But, clearly, precautions have to be taken to prevent the material from degrading prematurely.

A wide range of biodegradable plastics has been developed and promoted as an environmentally sensitive packaging solution. Most of the plastics, however, are biodestructible, rather than biodegradable. They are made by mixing special additives - usually cornstarch - with plastic polymers. This means that, although they do disintegrate over time, they do not break down completely, but instead leave tiny particles of polymer which may persist in the soil, possibly producing chemicals which may contaminate the soil or groundwater.

Biodegradable plastic is also less durable than conventional plastic, has less potential for re-use, and must be kept out of any plastics recycling stream because it has a destabilising effect. It is also more expensive to produce. For some uses, though, biodegradable plastic may be preferable to conventional plastic - if the plastic item will end up in the sewage system, for example.

A new generation of "bio-polymers", led by ICI's Biopol, could provide some solutions. These are produced from bacteria which manufacture natural polymers when grown on organic waste. These natural polymers can be removed and melted, moulded and recycled - just like oil-based plastic. Eventually, they decompose into carbon dioxide. High prices and limited versatility mean that applications in the short term will be restricted to spe-

▼ Designed by Gary Rowland Associates, this box for the French Connection fashion retailers not only packages shoes for distribution, but also acts as an effective point of sale stand. The box is made from a single sheet of pulp board, consisting largely of recycled fibres.

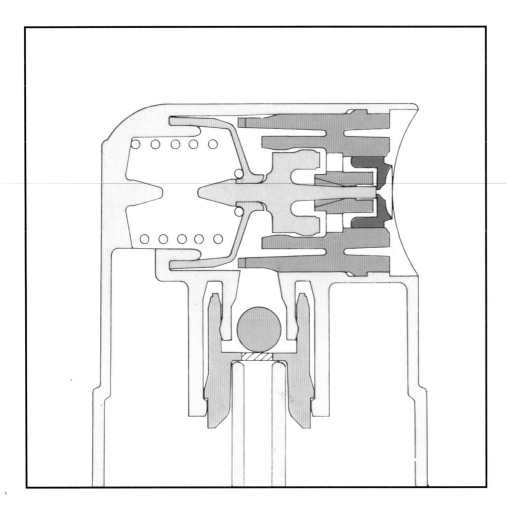

◄ ► The Atmosol aerosol system, from the British Technology Group, eliminates hazardous liquefied gas propellant by the use of compressed gases such as nitrogen or air. The major difference from a traditional aerosol is in the regulator, which replaces the button. The can is filled with liquid product, leaving a space at the top; this is pressurised with propellant gas. When the regulator is depressed (right), the valve at the top of the can opens, and gas pressure forces the product up the dip tube and out of the nozzle as a spray. A constant flow is achieved by a pressure-balanced diaphragm piston. The regulator at rest is shown on the left.

ciality uses such as medical apparatus or high-value toiletries. Other attempts to produce 100 per cent degradable plastic involve increasing the starch content, and using vegetable oils as the base ingredient.

"Natural plastics" may in the long term provide a realistic alternative to oil-based plastics, allowing the many benefits of plastics technology to be exploited without the problems that currently exist. In the short term, however, most interest appears to lie in recycling as the most practical way of managing the waste problem.

### Non-hazardous materials

Of course, packaging designers should try to avoid or minimise the use of any materials that are damaging to health or to the environment during production, use and eventual disposal. Additives such as cadmium have been found to pollute groundwater when packaging is degraded in landfill sites, and there are concerns about emissions or residues from some ingredients when they are incinerated. PVC has been singled out for special criticism recently; some European supermarkets ban its use in packaging, and many leading manufacturers are beginning to phase it out. Concerns focus on harmful

emissions of dioxin said to be given off when PVC is incinerated, and also on the chemical waste which results from its manufacture. The relative performance of PVC compared with other plastics is highlighted by PVC manufacturers, who emphasise its energy efficiency. Should emissions be demonstrated to be perfectly controllable, it is possible that PVC will be rehabilitated.

The fluctuating nature of concerns about the hazards of materials will inevitably cause problems for manufacturers and designers. Clearly, avoidance of substances or processes which may be more polluting or dangerous than feasible alternatives should be the guiding principle, even though issues may not be scientifically clear-cut. The "precautionary principle" provides an approach which minimises exposure to risk.

Scientific opinion is clear-cut, however, on the importance of avoiding materials which contain CFC gases, or which have used them during manufacture. Meat trays, egg boxes and many other packs can be made from alternative materials. Alternative propellants are available for aerosol use, if aerosols have to be the dispensing system. The need to avoid ozone-

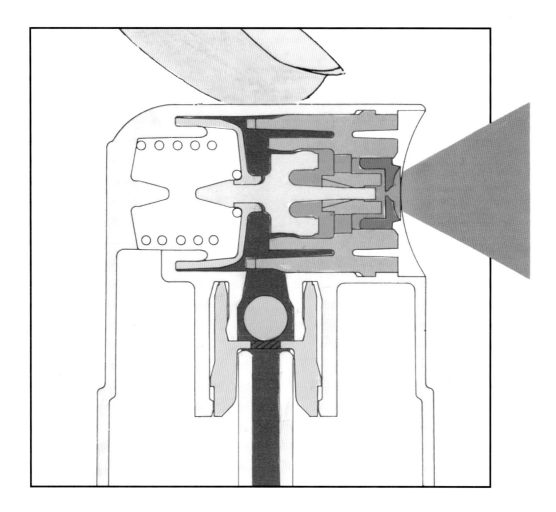

depleting propellants has stimulated a flood of innovative ideas in dispensing mechanisms, from the bag-in-can aerosol, to a refillable, self-pumping pump.

## Reducing the number of containers

Reducing the number of containers used per unit of product, or using bulk rather than individual containers, helps to minimise the amount of packaging used. Dispensing items which are regularly purchased and easy to store in larger sizes is one approach. Another is to find a way of delivering the product in bulk directly into the user's storage facility, an approach now widely used in the transfer of industrial ingredients such as cement or milk powder, which could have applications for consumer products through the growth of home delivery systems.

The ratio of product to packaging can also be changed through the use of product concentrates, which reduces the volume of the product and therefore the amount of packaging required. One obvious advantage for the manufacturer is that transport costs are reduced: diluting agents such as water are no longer con-

tained in the product, but are added by the consumer at time of use. For consumers, the packs are easier to handle and store. Concentrated detergents use fewer materials, less packaging and less energy in production.

## Secondary uses for packaging

In the interests of obtaining the greatest value out of the minimum resources, the possibilities of finding secondary uses for packs are being explored. Food packs that are resealable and dishwasher-proof are being proposed as re-usable food containers; a plastic soap package becomes a durable soap dish. However, this approach makes a significant contribution to overall waste reduction only if the pack fulfils a real need, and makes it unnecessary to buy another product. Cluttering up the house with packs may simply delay the disposal issue, as there is obviously a limit to how many containers people actually need. But for one-off purchases this approach may be worthwhile. A beautifully made package may be retained for a long time, either as an integral and valued part of the product inside, or as an attractive decorative item in its own right.

➤ A refillable and recyclable pressure dispensing system, designed by Packaging Innovation in the UK to replace aerosols. It comprises a double bag, made from recyclable PET film, containing the product and the flexible "airspring", which uses compressed air or carbon dioxide. The customer would buy the outer pack "shell", which might be made from a variety of materials, from recycled board to high-quality plastics, depending on the product. This has a "core" which, packaged very simply, would be replaced when the product is used up. One attraction of such a system for manufacturers is that it leads to customer loyalty: once customers have invested in the shell they would be likely to continue buying replacement cores.

## Packaging and litter

Packaging represents only a proportion of litter, but its visual effect is disproportionate. Packs designed for visual impact in a store unfortunately continue to have visual impact while lying on a street or in a field. While litter is a social problem which can be countered only by a change in individual attitudes, packaging design can help to minimise the damage caused.

Reducing the number of components in a pack can reduce the likelihood that small items, such as ring pulls, are dropped. Non-detachable tops mean that the larger item is more likely to be disposed of correctly, or is easier to clear up if is dropped.

Packaging litter can cause damage to wildlife. Plastic linking rings for multi-packs can prove hazardous to birds, for example, and plastic bags, if consumed by animals, can cause starvation by blocking the digestive system. Biodegradability and photodegradability have been proposed as ways of minimising these problems, providing that the materials are genuinely degradable. Photodegradability is most relevant to the litter problem, and may have some value, but is currently too expensive and impractical for most products. In the longer term, however, it may be possible to produce packaging material which can decompose quickly and safely, while still offering the product good protection when in use. It can be argued that making packaging more easily degradable will simply encourage litter, as items will be believed to disappear as if "by magic".

Eventually, the combination of packaging deposit schemes, improved litter bin availability and changes in public attitudes may reduce the litter problem. Until then, packaging designers may try incorporating bold symbols encouraging users to dispose of the pack carefully.

◄ Mobil Oil's "Drainmaster" is designed to solve the problem of what to do with the used oil in a car. The plastic container has two screw caps. Once the new oil has been poured in, the used oil can be poured from its collection tray into the larger, red, opening and the bottle re-closed. The used oil can then be delivered safely to an oil recycler.

# *case study*  *Detergent refills, Europe*

Detergent manufacturers are now considering both their packaging and the form of the products themselves, in order to reduce materials and energy use. In Europe, Procter and Gamble have led the way. The fabric conditioner Lenor, for example, has usually been sold in large plastic bottles which are thrown away when empty. Now a concentrated product is available, allowing a significant reduction in the amount of packaging materials needed, savings in transport costs and a more efficient use of supermarket shelf space. The concentrated product is packed in refill packs, such as a flexible plastic pouch or a carton; different packs have been used in different countries to take account of consumer preferences.

The pouch refill was initially launched in Germany. It contains one litre of concentrated product which the user pours into a four-litre bottle and then dilutes with water. The pouch is made from low-density polyethylene film, with a gusset in the base, which provides the necessary product protection and mechanical strength. Overall, the pouch consumes around 80 per cent less packaging material per litre of product than the regular four-litre bottle; it is over three times more space-efficient in transport and warehousing, and the display tray can merchandise ten pouches in the same space as three bottles. There is also a significant reduction in the direct product cost. Consumers find the pouch easy to carry, store and dispose of, compared with the old rigid plastic bottles, although pouring the refill pack into the bottle for dilution can result in spillages.

The carton is easier to pour from, and can also be used as a measuring device for diluting the concentrate. It is compact, and easy to open and to store. It uses around 65 per cent less packaging material per litre than the regular Lenor bottle. Like the pouch, it also gives savings in transport and warehousing. A distribution vehicle can carry three times as much in the refill pack as in the regular bottle, with consequent fuel savings.

Although the refill packs provide substantial advantages over one-use rigid plastic bottles, they themselves can only be used once, which might be regarded as wasteful. In some markets, we are likely to see a move towards returnable and re-usable bottles as the most environmentally sensitive option.

▼ Concentrated fabric softener in a sachet from Jeyes, UK. The contents are poured into a one-litre container, and diluted with water before use. The neck of the pack provides a convenient pouring spout.

▼ Refill cartons are
easy to pour into more
durable plastic bottles,
but they themselves
are discarded after one
use.

◄ These flexible
pouches, filled with
concentrate, consume
80 per cent less
packaging material per
litre of product than
regular bottles.

# *case study* *The Body Shop refill policy, UK*

▶ Perfumes are dispensed from large bottles, and can be added to base products, such as bath foam, without a proliferation of products on the shelf.

▼ The number of different pack sizes is kept to a minimum, with customers encouraged to buy the larger sizes.

The Body Shop is a franchised company with over four hundred outlets worldwide selling a wide range of toiletry products. The company adopts a non-exploitative approach to the environment, emphasising natural ingredients; simple, refillable packaging, and no testing of products on animals. Campaigning on environment issues is part of its ethos.

Minimal packaging includes cylindrical plastic bottles, with single walled caps, as standard. Plastic is used because it provides an effective barrier, and is robust, durable and light for distribution. It is also regarded as safer than glass, because of the potential danger if glass were to shatter into tiny particles.

But the virtues which make plastic so useful - its strength and durability - also create problems when it comes to disposal. The Body Shop considers that plastic packaging should be re-used wherever possible, and encourages its customers to bring bottles back for refilling by offering a small discount. Recycling is the next priority, with disposal considered as the last resort. Most products can be refilled, practically an unlimited number of times. The containers must be cleaned by the consumer before refilling, and hygiene standards require that they may be refilled only with the same product as before. This restriction is because of the permeable nature of plastic and the fact that only natural ingredients are used.

In 1990, the company launched an environmental campaign, "Once is Not Enough", to raise awareness of the need to reduce waste. The Refill Bar was the campaign's major focus, offering the best way to save resources.

To ease recycling, The Body Shop has minimised the number of different materials used for packaging, within the constraints of the need for compatibility between product and packaging.

➤ This poster dramatises the "re-use, recycle" message, advocating the extension of packaging life.

The clear bottles are made of PET (polyethylene terephthalate), and the opaque ones from HDPE (high-density polyethylene): both are recyclable materials. In future, the type of plastic will be identified on the pack to ease the sorting of waste, in anticipation of the development of recycling infrastructures. The Body Shop aims to recycle as much waste as possible, recovering materials such as cardboard and plastic film from the distribution system.

➤ Even the lorries used to distribute The Body Shop's products have a communication role.

# case study Procter and Gamble plastic recycling, UK

➤ The top picture shows the number of plastic bottles used by an average family in the course of one year, for laundry and cleaning products. If all of these bottles were made of recycled plastic, then the bottles in the lower picture show how many would be saved from going into a landfill site.

➤ Diagram showing the combination of new and recycled plastic in a detergent container.

**OUTER LAYER**
*COLORANT* IN *VIRGIN* MATERIAL

**MIDDLE LAYER**
*RECYCLE* MATERIAL

**INNER LAYER**
*VIRGIN* MATERIAL

Working in conjunction with its packaging suppliers and plastics recyclers, Procter and Gamble have developed new technology for using recycled post-consumer plastic waste, thus creating new market demand for the recycled plastic and providing a legitimate incentive for the expansion of facilities to collect and reprocess plastic bottles. Dr Frank Bossu, Associate Director of Product Development, said: "A major goal of this effort is to help build the recycling infrastructure needed to close the recycling loop."

The company will soon be using at least 25 per cent recycled HDPE (high-density polyethylene), a rigid plastic recycled from milk and water bottles which is used in bottles for fabric conditioners, such as Lenor in Europe and Downy in the USA, and for liquid detergents, such as Tide and Cheer in the USA. 100 per cent PET (polyethylene terephthalate), a clear plastic derived from soft drinks bottles, is used in the liquid cleaner bottle Spic 'n Span.

Mixed post-consumer plastic is collected in various ways: kerbside collection, bottle banks and separation in municipal reclamation schemes. It is shredded, flaked, washed and then separated by various mechanical processes into light and heavy fractions, the lighter fractions being mainly HDPE and polypropylene. It is then homogenised, melted, degassed and filtered before being formed into pellets which become the material used in the bottle production process.

The HDPE bottles are made by a process which combines new and recycled plastic in layers. There are two options. In one, the recycled plastic is sandwiched between inner and outer layers of new plastic; in the other, new plastic is used only on the inside, with recycled forming the outer layer. The interior layer of new plastic is judged necessary to avoid any possible contamination. These bottles have the same technical performance as bottles made entirely from virgin plastic, meeting all the same product safety, convenience and durability standards as well as handling, distribution and quality levels. Consumers will be able to identify these bottles as they will be marked with labels stating their recycled content.

If a family of four purchases recycled bottles for its laundry and cleaning requirements over a period of one year, approximately 22 half-gallon milk and water bottles and two-litre soft drinks bottles would be saved from going to landfill sites. The technology at present will use 25 per cent recycled HDPE, but it can incorporate levels of 50 per cent and perhaps more recycled plastic into HDPE packaging. The limiting factor in achieving the greater potential at present is the non-availability of recycling capacity, but many organisations are actively involved in building the infrastructure for effective collection of material for recycling.

▼ Recycled plastic by Lenor, used in the UK and Germany.

# *case study* *Yellow Design jewellery boxes, Germany*

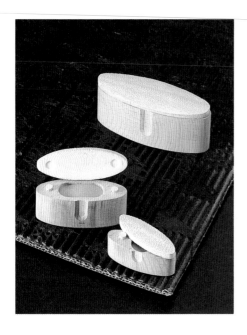

A criticism often made of the packaging of luxury goods such as cosmetics and jewellery is that more packaging is used than is needed to meet the requirements of functional performance. Günter Horntrich of Yellow Design in Germany set out to use minimal quantities of low-grade recycled board to pack jewellery. Simple boxes avoid the need for complex closures and instead use sliding covers or flaps. The boxes are also of regular shape and size to make packing in bulk easier.

Recycled carton and corrugated board were the principal materials used, creating an effect quite different from the traditional high-gloss approach. The insets within the boxes consist of recycled foam, made from the production waste of foam manufacturers, chopped into pieces and re-baked to give a multicoloured result.

These boxes replace plastic packs for rings, necklaces, watches and pins.

➤ Small boxes made of beech, with fishbone tops, are used to pack and store rings and pins.

➤ Necklaces and watches are presented in triangular boxes made from recycled carton board.

▼ Recycled plastic foam makes an unusual and attractive cushion to protect delicate jewellery.

# *case study*  *Berol Karisma pencils, UK*

Coloured pencils are usually packed in metal boxes, and colour identification is achieved through the use of a paint finish to the pencil which matches the colour of the lead. The Karisma brand of pencils, designed by UK consultancy Newell and Sorrell for Berol, broke with both these traditions.

The pencils are intended for use by illustrators, artists, designers and draughtsmen, and the design solution developed for the product and packaging keeps their interests very much to the fore: attention to detail, fine performance, and pleasure in use.

The intention of product and packaging was to give significant consideration to environment performance. The pencils remain unpainted, thus avoiding the use of an unnecessary secondary material and allowing the colour of the wood to be seen. The colour of the leads is revealed by cutting off the ends with an unusual champfered effect.

The unique "arts and crafts" look of the pencils had to be reflected in an appropriate packaging presentation, using simple craft materials. The card boxes are wrapped in textured, recycled paper; different coloured papers are used to denote pencil types. Recycled paper gives the pack a hand-crafted feel, an interesting texture and soft, unusual colours. Small points of detail on the design include hallmarks on the pencils, to denote quality, and brown paper document ties.

This approach is labour-intensive, but the use of unusual packaging materials and a very simple but aesthetically attractive presentation of the product give an end result which is unique and valuable - an item to be enjoyed and treasured.

▲ Champfered pencil ends make a beautiful detail, while providing the necessary colour identification.

➤ Thread document ties form the closures to the box, giving an attractive appearance and preventing the need for any extra material such as plastic.

▼ The presentation card box opens up to reveal the immaculately arranged pencils.

# 6    Printing and graphic design

The environment debate surrounding the use of paper and print has tended to focus on the use of recycled paper - the apparently simple, environment-conscious material choice. But there are several other significant areas of environment concern, right through the whole product life. Energy use, pollution, waste and land use have to be considered in the growing of raw materials, then there are the pulping and milling processes, the use and printing of the paper, and its eventual disposal.

➤ The French Paper Company in Michigan, USA, have developed a range of recycled papers called Speckletone, in reference to their distinctive texture and dappled appearance. The promotional material advertising their product and showing what can be achieved with it was designed by Duffy Design Group. Instead of making a standard-format brochure, they opted for a more durable book, attractive enough to be kept and valued. It combines various illustration styles, photography, die-cutting and thermography to create contrasting and imaginative effects. The highly textured paper creates a feeling as well as an image, and becomes an integral element of the design: inks combine to build up colour, while the unprinted areas are transformed from negative spaces into a positive visual element. The books have become collectors' pieces, ensuring a high profile for the company wherever Speckletone is sold.

Finding one's way through the complex maze of recycled papers is far from easy, because of the range of different grades and descriptions used. However, this area is one where designers should have considerable scope for including environment criteria in material selection and printing, and where the stimulus for innovative design is great.

## Raw material cultivation and extraction

Ninety per cent of the world's paper supply comes from wood, and paper products use about 10 per cent of the world's consumption of wood. Most of the wood comes from sustainably managed forests, and it is probably true that more trees are planted by the paper industry than are cut down. Trees are a renewable resource, and therefore harvesting them makes sense. However, there are several concerns about how trees are currently grown and felled.

● The intensive farming of single species, such as conifers in Scotland and eucalyptus in Portugal, can disrupt local ecologies and cause soil degradation.

● Some "old-growth" forests are felled for paper requirements, destroying habitats that have taken hundreds of years to evolve.

● Tropical rainforest has been cleared to make way for eucalyptus plantations.

● The "clearcutting" method of logging involves cutting down all trees in an area, even though not all will be used.

Responsibly managed forests, with appropriate trees grown in the right areas, are an important renewable resource, but the supply cannot be increased indefinitely.

Paper can be made from many other raw materials - the essential ingredient is cellulose, which is found in all plants.

● Leaf fibres - esparte, sisal and marillla.

● Seed fibres - cotton.

● Grass fibres - straw, maize stalks, cogan, bamboo and bagasse from sugar cane.

● Bast fibres - from the stems of flax, hemp and jute.

Until this century, materials such as straw, flax and rags were widely used, and there is growing interest again in these alternatives. Cotton fibres are separated from the seed when harvested, before the production of cottonseed oil: they contain a very pure form of cellulose, and can produce high quality papers, often with special strength or other characteristics. Of course, the growing of cotton is not without environmental problems, because of the widespread use of pesticides (see Chapter Seven, "Textile design").

The waste stubble from straw production, which in many countries would

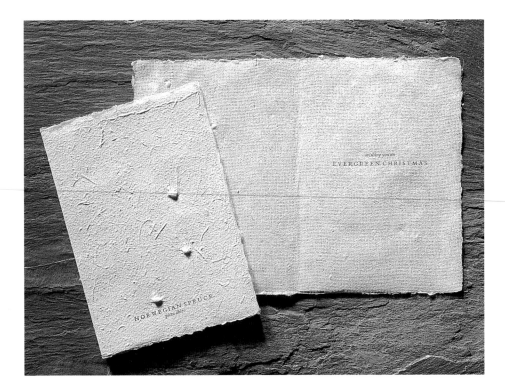

◄ Designed by London-based consultancy The Partners for the environmental campaigning group Earthlife, this Christmas card is intended to be planted: it has two pine tree seeds moulded into the paper. The card reinforces the organisation's campaign to preserve the world's forests.

➤ Roughly cut cotton rag paper and unusually bold colours create a striking Christmas card, designed by Jo Duffy for the Michael Peters Group.

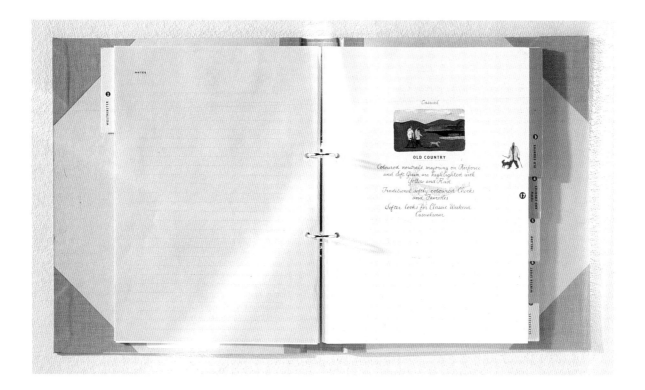

otherwise be burned, can be used to make straw paper, another high-quality product offering stiffness and opacity. There is even increasing interest in the production of paper from fruit and vegetable waste - such as banana skins!

Papers can also be made from cellulose-based man-made regenerated fibre, such as acetate. This gives an expensive, but highly durable product, suitable for applications such as banknotes.

At the moment, wood pulp appears to be the most economical raw material on an industrial scale, and the environment impact of tree cultivation can be controlled by careful husbandry. Other materials - especially those that use products which would otherwise go to waste - offer an interesting wealth of choice for the designer, and are well worth considering for special applications which can justify the cost (most are more expensive than wood-based papers).

The processes involved in paper production are much the same, whatever the basic ingredient.

Timber can be turned into pulp by two different processes. In the mechanical process, the tree is simply crushed to a pulp, using almost all of the tree. About half of the resultant material is fibres, with much of the rest being lignin, a stiffening material which binds the fibres together in the tree. The presence of lignin, which is light-sensitive, means that the resultant paper turns brown in sunlight, and it is therefore used for short-life products such as newspapers and for brown cardboard

boxes. Mechanical crushing is a highly energy-intensive operation.

The alternative process is chemical pulping, which involves treating wood chips with chemicals to remove the resins. The lignin is separated off and used as fuel. About 50 per cent of the total tree therefore becomes pulp.

## Milling

During the paper-making process, from pulping through to bleaching and converting, a wide variety of chemicals is used, and some end up released as waste in effluent. One of the most publicised pollution issues concerning chemicals in pulping and processing is the release of chlorine-related compounds such as dioxins, caused by the use of chlorine bleaching to enhance the whiteness of the paper. Some of these substances are now known to be highly toxic.

The tiny amount of dioxin which may be left in paper is thought to be highly unlikely to cause any human health problems, but if dioxins are discharged as waste into the environment they may be hazardous to wildlife, and they remain in the environment for a long time. Whatever the level of risk, it now makes more sense for chlorine to be replaced as a bleaching agent by hydrogen peroxide, and this has already been done by several major paper manufacturers.

Optical brightening agents, dyes, slimicides and substances to strengthen the paper can be added during processing.

▲ "Trends" file, produced each season by the garment buying team for company use at the UK-based chain Marks and Spencer, to illustrate the current fashion themes. For autumn 1990, themes of nature and hand-crafting predominate. A mix of recycled papers was chosen to help convey the desired tone; the relaxed surface of the paper, together with the hand-drawn lettering, echo the soft styling of the clothes.

The production of paper uses vast quantities of energy, which can be reduced by half if waste paper is used. Water consumption is also high, although most modern plants recycle as much as possible.

In most countries the paper industry is investing heavily in pollution-control technology to reduce effluent problems, but many mills exceed the discharge limits granted to them.

## Virgin or recycled?

To recycle paper, waste paper is softened in steam and water to separate out the cellulose fibres. Contaminants such as staples are filtered out, and the pulp can then be used for cardboard or for low-quality paper. Waste paper usually contains ink. To produce higher-quality recycled paper, the waste paper is put through a de-inking process, where surface-active chemicals and soaps absorb the inks during a flotation process. The fibres are then usually bleached, with a chlorine or hydrogen peroxide bleach. These processes produce an effluent, which must be controlled.

The higher the proportion of secondary fibre used, the weaker the paper will be, because of the loss of cellulose fibres. This is why paper cannot be recycled indefinitely, and why a combination of virgin and secondary fibre is frequently used for paper which will be printed.

Recycled paper is a catch-all phrase, which actually covers a broad spectrum of very different materials. Over time, we should see detailed labelling of papers, indicating what the recycled proportion is, and what grade of waste is used. Waste paper may be derived from several sources.

- Virgin paper which is wasted during paper production, often known as "mill broke".

- Unprinted waste paper sent back to the mill by converters and printers, as off-cuts and waste.

- Printed virgin material, which can include high-quality office waste.

- Low-grade waste, which can include newspapers, packaging and cardboard.

The supply of low-grade waste, which is collected enthusiastically by households, frequently exceeds demand; the opposite is now true for high-grade. Low-grade paper is used to make outer packaging and cardboard, and is beginning to be used for products like toilet tissue, but most recycled papers are made from high-quality, pre-consumer waste. Many recycled papers could contain higher quantities of lower-grade waste, but manufacturers often prefer to offer recycled paper that looks indistinguishable from virgin paper, which demands the use of the highest grade of waste.

The use of recycled paper - particularly low-grade recycled paper - is desirable from an environmental perspective for several reasons.

- Making paper from waste paper saves significant amounts of energy and water compared with virgin paper.

- Much paper is now disposed of through landfill sites; with space running out and costs increasing, waste minimisation makes sense.

- Using recycled paper will reduce the overall demand for trees, which might prevent the spread of intensive forestry into new, inappropriate areas.

- The amount of chemicals used in making recycled paper should be less than for virgin paper, although this is not always the case.

Recycled paper is therefore preferable in many ways to virgin paper, but there are some drawbacks. It is less consistent in performance and appearance than virgin paper; it can contain substances such as

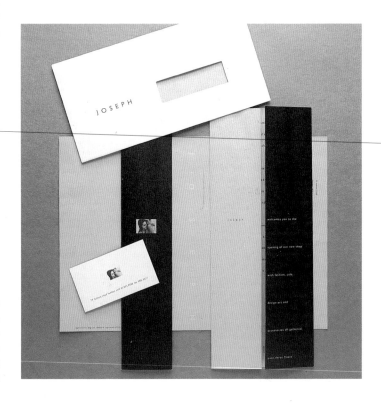

▼ Sugar paper was the choice for corporate literature designed for Joseph by N2 in London. It was selected for its texture, which gives a distinctive end result, rather than for any environmental considerations. The background is also sugar paper.

➤ Booklet designed in 1988 by Neville Brody and Jon Wozencroft to accompany a music album being distributed in the Soviet Union to launch the environmental organisation Greenpeace. The design had to take into consideration the limitations of Russian printing; the typeface, for example, had to be Helvetica. A non-chlorine bleached paper was selected, in line with other Greenpeace publications. Although originally intended to be printed in the USSR, the booklet was eventually printed in Britain. The album sold 2 million records and I million tapes in the USSR, and was then repackaged for other countries with different imagery in design to reflect different cultures. The background to the booklet is khadi paper, made from lokta (see pages 130-33).

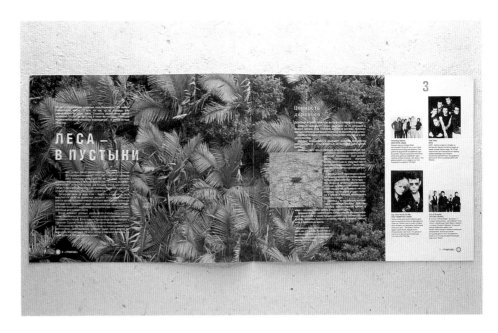

◄ ▼ Printed proof sheets of postcards by Anderson Fraser, using images by contemporary designers and illustrators. The printing is on recycled paper, to show the high quality which can be achieved; each image will be mounted on recycled board. ▮

inks which mean that it is not as clean as virgin paper; and the damaging of fibres reduces its strength. It also performs differently from virgin paper in printing. High cost has been cited as a drawback, but this is due to the small scale of reclamation and production rather than to the inherent costliness of the process.

There are many new paper products which contain non-paper ingredients; laminates, hydrocarbon films and synthetic fibres make paper hard to recycle. Another problem is latex adhesive particles - often from self-adhesive envelopes - which, when recycled, adversely affect paper quality and printability.

## Designing and printing with recycled paper

Recycled paper and board have different technical and visual qualities from virgin material, and these must be understood by the designer right from the start of the design process. The choice of material will affect the performance and appearance of the design, and so the two ingredients must be considered together.

The wide range of recycled paper gives a choice of textures, colours and printing characteristics. Achieving an end result comparable to high-quality virgin paper may be difficult with all but the highest grade of recycled paper, but it is now possible to produce fine four-colour printing on recycled paper to a very high standard. However, the use of lower-grade paper should be considered by the designer for the interesting effects which can be achieved.

In general, recycled papers are more absorbent, have a more uneven surface than virgin, and are less white. The higher dot gain resulting from the absorbency can give a soft-edged image with a sepia effect - like that seen in old photographs - and the printed image can seem duller, with colours lacking brilliance. If ink remains in the paper from its previous use, print may have a lack of "punch", but this can create an attractive effect.

Designer and printer have to be aware of print characteristics such as opacity, smoothness, absorbency, runnability and rigidity early on, and make sure the reproduction and printing processes are modified accordingly. Cylinder pressure may have to be adjusted, and print speed is likely to be lower; inks must be carefully selected as well.

This considered approach calls for a dialogue between designer and printer, and for time to be spent selecting the most appropriate combination of material and design style. The colour printing process must be undertaken methodically, with proofing done on the paper which will eventually be used.

Recycled papers can work particularly well as "negative space" surrounding printed matter, as the appearance of the paper alone can add interest and impact.

Designers can play an important role in changing public perceptions of quality. The view is still widely held that shiny white virgin paper, covered with varnish, epitomises quality, and many companies are reluctant to use recycled paper in their packaging, literature or corporate stationery for that reason. This means that paper is often over-specified - much higher grades are used than would actually be required in terms of functional performance. Concerns about the appearance of recycled paper can be addressed in two ways: by the use of higher-quality recycled paper which looks very similar to virgin paper, and by demonstrating, through imaginative design, how lower-quality paper can be aesthetically appealing as well as environmentally sound. Unnecessary over-specification of materials quality may come to be seen as bad design in the future, indicative of a lack of understanding and imagination.

There may be applications for which recycled paper is simply not suitable. In these cases a non chlorine-bleached virgin wood paper, or a paper made from an alternative such as straw, should be used instead.

## Inks and solvents

During the printing process, solvents and dyes may cause the risk of damage to the environment or may be a health hazard to workers. Many types of solvent are used as bases for inks for gravure, flexographic and letterpress printing; their evaporation ensures that the ink dries quickly. But solvents can be dangerous to health if inhaled in too high a concentration, causing potential problems for print workers, and their emission into the atmosphere contributes to the build-up of unwanted gases.

The alternative is to use water-soluble inks. These are cleaner and vapourless, but tend to take longer to dry, which means that drying equipment has to be modified or the printing slowed down. Efforts are being made to develop new additives which will speed up the drying process, but these may affect the quality of the end result.

Vegetable oil-based inks are being introduced in some newspaper printing as an alternative to petroleum-based inks. The main motive for this is the better

 のは 日黒区美術館

How to wrap 5 eggs

5つの卵はいかにして包まれたか

日本の伝統パッケージ展

10月9日〔日〕
11月6日〔日〕

▲ Poster for a packaging design exhibition in Tokyo, designed by Kijuro Yahagi using straw as an alternative to paper. When combined with a small sheet of paper printed with the exhibition details, it produces an original and attractive effect. This choice of material was commercially acceptable for an edition of 1,000 posters. Yahagi won the Warsaw Graphic Design prize in 1990.

printers are therefore likely to use solvent-based inks for some time yet. If solvents cannot be avoided, care should be taken to ensure that the chemicals are disposed of carefully, and emissions reduced to a minimum by using solvent burners. Designers should request information from printers about their ingredients and processes and about how they handle chemical disposal, as part of the procedure of selecting a supplier.

## Resource consumption

Resource minimisation is always the aim of environment-conscious designers, and there are a variety of ways in which the quantity of paper used can be reduced.

### Efficient use of space

In some applications, designers can condense information into a reduced format, through the imaginative use of typeface and layout, thus saving paper. When this is done for very large production runs, the savings can be very considerable - in paper, energy and waste. The saving in paper achieved by the redesign of British Telecom's telephone directories is significant, considering that 24 million books are produced each year, consuming 80,000 trees (see pages 128-9).

### Product life

The potential life span of a product should be taken into consideration at the stage of design and material choice. Timetables, direct mail, even paperback novels have a very short life, and can therefore be made from poorer quality paper than, say, encyclopaedias, which have to be very durable. The design of paper products for instant disposability might be questioned. Direct mail consumes paper resources, but only a tiny proportion of mailings are ever read or acted upon. Perhaps the answer lies in much better designed, more original offerings which might not go unread, or alternatively in the use of other forms of communication which are better targeted.

colour brightness and sharper dot achieved, and their improved rub resistance, which prevents print coming off on to the hands. At the moment, vegetable oil-based inks tend to be used as an additive rather than on their own, but there may be increasing acceptance of them as complete alternatives to solvent-based inks.

The use of heavy metal-based pigments in inks, such as cadmium and lead, has been criticised because of their pollutant effect in effluent, and alternatives are being sought. However, it is difficult to match their unique colour and opacity properties.

The environment-conscious option in printing appears to lie with water-based and vegetable oil-based inks, and the designer should request these wherever possible. However, new equipment may be required to handle them, and many

Sometimes, pieces of literature are designed to be rapidly superseded by others: a company brochure, for example, may be replaced every few months. There may be opportunities to replace a succession of clearly "disposable" brochures with one that is designed to last. If the information is not to be quickly superseded, and a long functional life span is possible, a more durable concept could reduce the need for replacement brochures or multiple copies. Duffy Design in the USA have produced a book for Dicksons instead of a standard-format brochure. It is highly

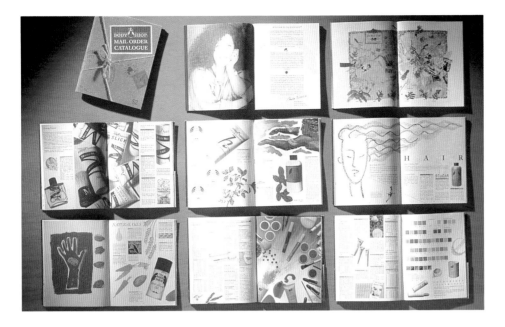

◄ London-based design consultancy Newell and Sorrell and printers Anderson Fraser made recycled paper a special component of the design of the 1989 Body Shop mail order catalogue. Eight different colours, four different weights of stock and five different textures were used. Close collaboration produced successful results despite the use of design features normally avoided with recycled paper, such as small type size, images across gutters and complicated tint-laying. The printing procedures were carefully adjusted to minimise the problems of printing on rougher, more absorbent paper. A range of 72 cosmetics colours had to be shown, with very subtle differences between colours: after tests, recycled paper proved more accurate than virgin, retaining softness while giving excellent colour reproduction.

functional in demonstrating the work of the company, but also attractive and durable, making sure that customers value it and keep it. Its distinctiveness also ensures that the company stands out strongly among competitors.

### Alternatives to paper

Paper is not necessarily the ideal way of storing information. If subjected to continued, hard use - such as with reference books - the material will become worn and tattered. New technology can provide alternatives for information storage. The use of CD-rom (a compact disc with a read-only memory) provides an electronic tool for infinite access to information in a format that suffers little physical degradation. Vast amounts of information can be stored in a tiny area. While the "paperless office" has proved to be a myth so far, as people continue to prefer to communicate on paper, electronic data storage will spread rapidly, eventually reducing paper requirements.

Electronic data storage is currently being used for design manuals. Instead of a large paper-based reference system, specifications can be stored on computer disk, allowing for greater accuracy and easier updating.

### The design decision

There are some general guidelines for the environment-conscious literature designer.

● Wherever possible, use recycled paper, selecting the highest percentage of secondary fibre consistent with functional and aesthetic requirements.

● Consider the paper type at the earliest stage of design development, to ensure that the design and paper are sympathetic.

● Assess whether the quantity of paper required can be minimised through layout and typography.

● Avoid papers which have been chlorine bleached; try unbleached paper, or paper bleached with hydrogen peroxide instead.

● Try water-soluble or vegetable oil-based inks as an alternative to solvent-based inks.

● Ask suppliers how they deal with effluent from the various chemical processes used throughout the paper-making and printing cycle.

● Remember that paper made out of alternative materials can sometimes be an interesting and attractive alternative to wood-derived paper.

▼ Exhibition catalogue for the Venice Biennale of 1990, designed by Kijuro Yahagi. For the covers, he scorched the pattern straight on to the paper, without the use of ink, reflecting a technique used by one of the artists in the exhibition. They were scorched by hand, giving each one an individual pattern.

# *case study* *The Body Shop annual report 1988, UK*

▲ The front cover is imaginatively layered, with recycled paper on the outside and virgin paper on the inside to give a smooth surface for a sharp image. This contrasts with the softer image on the right hand page, which is printed on a more absorbent surface.

In keeping with the company's commitment to good environment performance, The Body Shop's 1988 annual report was designed to be printed on environmentally considered papers. Designers Neville Brody and Jon Wozencroft were given a free hand, and developed a theme of contrasting papers, textures and photographic techniques through the use of non-bleached and recycled papers. Four contrasting types of paper were selected after an extensive search; such papers had not previously been used for important company documents.

The cover is made from white-backed chipboard, which is usually restricted to packaging boxes for items like shoes. The two layers, of recycled and virgin materials, offer two completely different printing surfaces. The recycled side, on the outside, gives a minimal, grainy look, contrasting with the virgin side, which folds out to provide a surface for bold, sharp photographic imagery.

Inside the book, sugar paper, in several colours with an absorbent surface, is used to create subtle, sensual imagery from photography. 100 per cent recycled brown wrapping paper offers two surfaces - one matt and one gloss - while matt, non-chlorine-bleached paper provides more contrast of texture and colour.

The report is an early example of the use of environmentally conscious paper to create a high-profile, prestigious company report. It successfully challenges the traditional approach which assumes that quality must be conveyed through high gloss and brilliant white paper. The inherent properties of recycled paper have been exploited to the full to give a wide range of interesting and innovative effects.

◀ Brown paper provides a distinctive background with its laid lines. All of these pictures of the catalogue have been photographed on a background of Kraft brown wrapping paper.

➤ Sugar paper gives a rich, soft image.

# *case study* *British Telecom phonebooks, UK*

British Telecom manufactures 24 million telephone directories each year, consuming around 80,000 trees. Laid end to end, the print run would stretch from London to Singapore. Any saving in the size of the directories would thus produce a significant saving in resources. British Telecom, working with designers Colin Banks and John Miles, carried out a research programme to see if, by redesigning the typeface and layout of the directories, they could reduce their size.

Because each entry must take at least one line, the major way of saving space is to reduce the space taken by each letter and the spaces between words. This produced a saving of 8 per cent, and at the same time gave a more readable result.

The change from three to four columns a page was made possible by the space economy of the type, and by dropping the repeat surname and the exchange codes. Scanning columns of names is now quicker, as the differences between them, rather than the similarities, are most apparent.

Directories are printed at very high speed, so they risk being under-inked. With smaller type, under-inking could lead to a readability problem. A typeface was selected which had a strong, distinct letter form.

Savings of paper in excess of 10 per cent have been achieved, and market research has shown that 80 per cent of users prefer the new format. This is the kind of practical contribution that good graphic design can make to improving environment impact, reducing costs and increasing user satisfaction. The redesign won the Green Product Award, a UK prize sponsored by the petrol company Shell.

▲ The redesigned phonebook provided a good opportunity for corporate image-building, with this advertisement aimed at environment-conscious consumers.

➤ A comparison of different designs, showing how reduced letter- and word-spacing and condensed type contribute to a 10 per cent space saving.

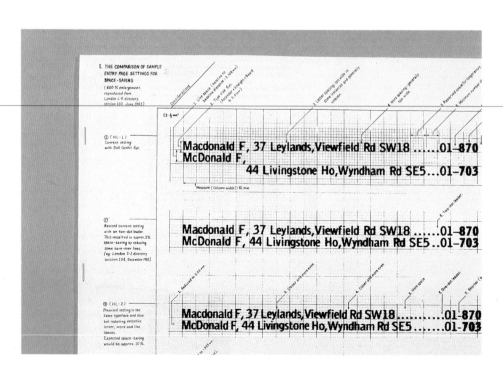

◀ Each letter was carefully redesigned to save space, while retaining clarity.

▼ The new layout (top) fits four instead of three columns across a page, and the names and numbers are more readable.

**547  Hodges D**  Where no exchange is shown it is BIRMINGHAM (021–)  **Hodgkiss J  547**

**16  Appleby L**  PLYMOUTH ASSESSMENT  **Armstrong A  16**

# *case study* *Handmade papers, India, Nepal and the UK*

➤ **Handmade khadi cotton rag paper from South India.**

◄ **Produced by Maureen Richardson on a craft basis, these papers illustrate the contrasting textures that can be achieved with recycled and plant paper. Pictured clockwise from the top left corner: recycled printers' waste with straw; pure rush; recycled printers' waste with coloured thread; pure straw and manilla; recycled printers' waste with onion.**

➤ A selection of papers illustrating the opacity of these unusual materials. Pictured clockwise from the top left on a background of tsasho paper made from lokta bark are: pure flax, made by Maureen Richardson in the UK; tissue from the kozo plant bark from Japan; tissue from recycled lokta from Nepal.

A wide variety of hand-crafted papers, made from recycled or plant materials, are now available for designers to use. These papers provide interesting opportunities for literature and packaging design, where small runs are required and a unique effect is desirable. Although many handmade papers are not appropriate for modern, high-speed printing presses, they can give excellent results if printed carefully.

Handmade papers are produced throughout the Third World, where in many places this traditional industry is being revived. The Body Shop, based in the UK, is sponsoring a paper-making operation near Katmandu in the Himalayas.

The papers are formed sheet by sheet, on a woven cloth or a covered rectangular frame. In both India and Nepal the sheet is formed by pouring pulp into the mould. Water helps the pulp to spread in an even film over the surface of the mould, and drains out when the mould is lifted. In Northern India, papermakers use a "chapri" - a paper mould made of grass stems strung together, which gives the papers their characteristic "laid" pattern. In Nepal, papers are made in a Japanese way on a "su" mould. In both Nepal and Bhutan, the paper is sun-dried on the mould and then peeled off when dry, whereas in India the sheet of wet paper is laid on woollen felt and pressed, then hung to dry. Many of these papers use only waste products for raw material, although some incorporate plant fibres.

 Pictured on natural recycled lokta paper from Nepal, this paper, which is pleated when wet then dried in the sun, has been mounted on a thicker paper base to give added strength. It is used to make decorative, colourful gift packs for The Body Shop.

◄ Plant papers made by Mara Amats provide stiff materials for packaging due to their long fibres. Pictured clockwise from the top left on a background of papyrus paper are: pure live banana fibre; pure dried banana fibre; recycled paper with onion; pure maize.

Maureen Richardson, based in England, produces a selection of papers made from waste paper and plants; straw, wool and flax are used to give texture and colour. In India, the basic raw material for contemporary handmade paper is "khadi" - cotton in the form of rags and waste material from tailors; the long fibres give the paper great strength. Other materials can be added to give colour and texture - recycled jute and hemp sacking to give gunny paper, banana leaf waste to give banana paper, and waste sugar cane fibre to give bagasse. Mara Amats produces papers wholly made from grasses and banana plants. Other materials used include rice straw and rice husk, dried strands of algae, tea dust and wool.

Many of these papers provide good material for packaging, because of their stiffness and strength. The natural colours of, for example, the water hyacinth weed can provide strong visual impact.

In Nepal, paper is also made from the bark of the lokta tree. This can be stripped without killing the plant, and can be re-harvested within four years.

▼ Packaging material made from banana and paper made from water hyacinths in Nepal provide a creative opportunity for designers, as seen in these packs by The Body Shop for pot pourri, and in the gift-wrapped soap from The Conran Shop, decorated with a bodhi leaf.

# 7     Textile design

The textiles designer trying to be environment-conscious faces some confusing choices. Assessing the environment impact of textiles really requires a cradle-to-grave approach, in which all aspects of production, use and disposal are carefully considered. The materials themselves, and the processes used to produce them, are the major determinants of environment impact.

At first glance, it might appear that sticking to natural fibres, and using vegetable dyes rather than chemicals, would ensure minimal environment impact. But even the production of natural fibres such as cotton can cause major environment damage. Pesticides and fertilisers are used in large quantities in cotton growing, and intensive cotton production can exhaust the fertility of the soil. It is much less energy-consuming, however, than the production of a synthetic fibre such as polyester.

Although a raw material may appear to be environmentally attractive, the processes used on it can be less benign. Fibres such as viscose, made from wood pulp-derived cellulose, come from a renewable source, and are biodegradable. But the process used to turn wood pulp into fabric involves the use of potentially harmful chemicals.

Textile production is split into different stages: fibre and yarn production, bleaching and dyeing, cloth assembly and finishing. The different raw materials take various routes to the bleaching and dyeing stage, after which the processes can be similar for different types of cloth.

## Fibre and yarn production

Textiles are manufactured from three basic categories of raw material: natural fibres; regenerated fibres derived from natural sources, and man-made synthetic fibres derived from petro-chemicals. But although materials may be produced very differently, they all have some detrimental environment effects if produced on an industrial scale.

### Natural fibres

Cotton, linen, wool and silk are the principal natural fibres used in textile production. Each one raises environmental concerns.

Cotton is grown with the aid of fertilisers, pesticides and fungicides, to boost yields and protect the plants from highly destructive insects and disease. It has been estimated that almost a quarter of the world's use of pesticides goes into the production of cotton. The shorter growing cycle of flax, used for linen, means that it needs much lower quantities of these items. Fertilisers and pesticides can seep into streams and rivers, causing a build-up of micro-organisms that deplete the water of oxygen and so starve out the plants and animals that live there. The water may also simply become too toxic for them to survive. Of course, the chemicals can eventually find their way into the drinking water supply of animals and people. In India, the pesticides used for cotton production, such as DDT, may well be banned in other countries.

Because some insects are becoming more resistant to general-purpose pesticides, alternatives are being developed. One interesting route is to use pheromones to control the breeding of pests and repel them. But such biological controls may be effective only for a specific species in a particular location, making them very expensive to develop.

Cotton is an important cash crop for the Third World, and takes up 5 per cent of the world's productive land. Intensive production requires a great deal of water, and can make surrounding areas arid.

The production of wool also, perhaps surprisingly, involves the use of pesticides

➤ Wood fibre is woven into a warp of strong cotton to produce "Papertex" carpets, which are hard-wearing and easy to clean. Finnish designer Ritva Puotila aims for simplicity and economy of materials, producing results which seem to draw inspiration from Japanese as well as Scandinavian traditions.

▲ Shawls made in Nepal from the wool of the pashmina goat, woven with silk from China. Part of an aid programme, these products build on local skills, adapting them for more commercial use: shawls in the area have traditionally been made only with cotton. The darker shawl is dyed with a vegetable-based dye; the lighter one is unbleached and undyed. They are very soft, with a lovely sheen, and could potentially be produced in much larger quantities.

and fertilisers. They may be used on the plants that the animals eat, and to produce animal feed. Pesticides are also applied to wool during the sheep-dipping process, to prevent infestation by parasitic insects. Pesticide residues left on wool after the cleaning process are tiny, and not harmful to people; but the lanolin - the grease extracted from the wool - may be contaminated, and therefore unsuitable for use in toiletries and pharmaceuticals. The effluent from the cleaning process can be highly polluting and must therefore be strictly controlled.

Although sheep tend to graze on land which is not rich enough for other forms of agriculture, their presence can keep the soil poor and prevent the natural development of plant life.

Animal welfare may also be a concern in wool production. Sheep are often bred to carry unnaturally heavy coats of wool, which can cause them discomfort. During the shearing process they are routinely cut and distressed, and skin may be sliced off around the tail area to prevent infestation by maggots.

The production of silk might also appear cruel. Farmed silkworm moths are asphyxiated in their cocoons once they have spun their silk thread. However, wild silk, which accounts for some 15 per cent of silk production, allows the worm to escape, having spun its cocoon.

Fabric can also be produced from a wide variety of natural materials. The fibres from pineapple and banana leaves can be spun into thread, and turned into fabrics similar to linen and silk. This is a very time-consuming and skilled process, currently done by hand in countries like the Philippines.

### Regenerated fibres

Regenerated fibres such as rayon, viscose and acetate are derived from cellulose, the basic building block of plants. This is extracted from wood pulp, from trees like the eucalyptus and spruce, which are fast-growing and cultivated for harvesting. Although wood is a renewable resource, care must be taken not to grow trees intensively in inappropriate areas, because of problems of soil degradation and erosion.

Once the cellulose has been extracted, it is mixed with chemicals such as carbon disulphide and sulphuric acid to form a spinning solution. The cellulose base of these fibres gives them an attractive natural origin, and they can offer an environmentally responsible alternative to natural fibres if they are processed with great care.

▲ Cotton yarn, coated with fibre from the Japanese banana plant "basho", is woven to produce a durable, linen-like fabric. Designed by Reiko Sudo and manufactured by the Nuno Corporation in Tokyo, it demonstrates the imaginative use of alternative materials for textiles. Environmental benefits depend, as in every case, on the chemicals and processes used during manufacturing.

◄ Cotton garments made in a Gambian village as part of an aid programme to create work for women. The cotton is home-produced and home-spun. It is quite untreated, and the designs show how well the features of uneven texture can be exploited to create a beautiful effect.

◀ ▶ Acetate is made from cellulose derived from wood pulp, a renewable natural resource. Cool and comfortable to wear, it can be used to create many different effects of texture and colour. Georgina Godley's designs, entitled "Willow Tree" (right) and "Silver Birch Tree" (left) have a theatrical quality. Iridescent velvets, chevron pleats and slinky lengths of chain-mail demonstrate the versatility of this fabric, which has been promoted as a long-term alternative to silk.

## Synthetic fibres

Synthetic fibres include nylon, polyester and acrylic. They are predominantly oil-based, and can therefore be criticised for depleting a scarce, non-renewable resource. However, they account for only a tiny amount of oil (23,000 of the 57 million barrels used every day), and therefore do not represent a major drain.

Their manufacture is energy-intensive, however, and involves the use of a wide range of chemical processes which can, if not strictly controlled, produce emissions which are harmful to the atmosphere or water. They can take hundreds of years to biodegrade; research is being carried out with the aim of speeding this up. Because they are oil-derived, they could, at the end of their life, be used to produce fuel.

## The design decision

Most environmentalists argue strongly in favour of the use of natural fibres on the grounds that they are renewable, long-lasting and non-allergenic. But even natural fibres can cause problems at the production stage, and the designer should seek out suppliers who are trying to produce in the least damaging way. "Organic" or "green" cotton, for example, is now emerging on a commercial scale (see pages 146-7).

For some uses, regenerated or synthetic fibres may be preferable. Regenerated fibres, in particular, offer a real alternative to the finest natural materials such as silk. Viscose and acetate can be comfortable and versatile, and are favourites of leading fashion designers.

While it is often difficult to find reliable information on how these are produced, a good indicator is the manufacturer's overall reputation for environment performance. Is the company always hitting the headlines for discharging effluent into rivers, or is it a leading innovator in developing better products and processes? Courtauld's new fabric Tencel is a regenerated fibre for which the only major effluent is water (see pages 148-9), and many other manufacturers are trying to reduce the environment impact of their production process. Details of a company's and a product's environment performance should always be requested from suppliers, to enable a judgement to be made.

## Textile manufacture

Many different substances may be used during the manufacture of yarn and fabric. Bleaching, dyeing, mercerising, proofing and stabilising are just some of the processes a fabric may go through to give it the desired strength, appearance and texture. During these treatments, the most important environmental factor is the pollution that is possible if the correct controls are not used. Some of the substances used, like waxes and starches, may be relatively harmless and biodegradable except in high concentrations, but others may be toxic.

Pollution caused by the discharge of chemicals is one of the major "controllable" environment problems surrounding textile production, and in many countries tougher and tougher laws are being introduced to try to minimise it. More effective pollution-abatement equipment is expensive, however, and not all countries have the same standards. There is therefore a temptation to have fabric processed in countries where controls are lax and overall production costs are low. The pollution problem is then simply exported, often to Third World countries.

### Sizing and bleaching

Before cotton is woven, starch or synthetic size is used to lubricate and strengthen the fibres during weaving. This is washed off when the cotton has been woven. Discharging large quantities of starch into rivers can stimulate the growth of oxygen-depleting micro-organisms, despite the fact that it is biodegradable; synthetic size needs to be carefully controlled. Very large quantities of water are used to clean and bleach silk; this both wastes and contaminates water.

Most natural, and some synthetic, fibres are bleached before being dyed.

Bleaching with chlorine-based chemicals can cause the release of harmful organo-chlorides into rivers and seas; a much safer form of bleaching uses hydrogen peroxide, which does not result in toxic by-products.

### Dyeing

Dyeing can be carried out at a number of stages in the production process from fibre to end product, and involves a wide variety of chemicals. Many dyes are not easily biodegradable, and are difficult to recover in effluent controls. They can pass through into rivers, where they can cause problems by preventing light reaching plant life.

Wool dyeing can involve the use of heavy metals, such as chromium, copper and zinc, which are water pollutants. New techniques are being developed by the International Wool Secretariat to prevent residual levels of metal in effluent.

Single-colour dyes can be recycled, whereas multi-colour printing produces a waste product of useless grey sludge.

Other chemicals may be used as part of the dyeing process. Solvents may be required, and the corrosive discharges from dye plants are neutralised with powerful acids. Some synthetic fibres, like polyamide, take dyes more readily than natural fibres, which results in less waste of the dye during the process.

Do natural plant dyes offer a realistic alternative? Their use avoids the problems of chemical effluents, but there are several drawbacks. Plant dye content is only around 5 per cent, so vast numbers of plants would have to be specially cultivated to supply the textile industry, and most of the plant would go to waste. Natural dyes do not match the performance of synthetic dyes in terms of colour-fastness and consistency, and cannot be used on some synthetic fabrics.

Attempts are now being made to produce "natural" dyes industrially through a fermentation process, with waste products being used as organic fertiliser.

### Finishing treatments

After weaving or knitting, most natural fabrics are cleaned (or "scoured") a second time to shrink the fabric and fluff up the fibres. This process also produces potentially damaging effluent. Synthetic and regenerated fibres are set into place by heating under tension - a highly energy-intensive process.

Many fabrics are treated with special finishes to give them valuable properties, like water-proofing, crease-resistance or shrink-proofing. The use of formalde-hyde, a carcinogen, has given rise to some concerns for human health, particularly that of workers involved in the production process. The pesticides used to moth-proof natural fibres may cause health problems as well as producing effluent which is toxic to aquatic life. Mercerisation, a process often used on cotton to give it a sheen, uses substances like liquid ammonia and caustic soda which must be carefully controlled. Synthetic fibres tend to need less finishing, as the fabric itself can be specially constructed to make it crease-resistant, for example.

### The design decision

Unbleached, undyed, untreated fabric can of course be used. Cream, unbleached cotton is already used for clothes and furnishings, but the opportunities in aesthetic terms are limited. Natural dyes can give attractive and interesting effects, although absolute precision should not be expected in terms of colour matching batches.

The mechanical design of the yarn and the way the fabric is woven can actually reduce the need for chemical finishing treatments. An interesting example is "green cotton", in which the yarn in the cotton jersey is given a special twist: the resultant substance and springiness stops the material from spiralling and twisting. Close partnerships between scientists, textile designers and fashion designers may produce many interesting new approaches. Once again, good environmental solutions may lie in considering the early-stage, technical aspects of material production as critical components of the design process.

Where dyes and special treatments are needed, the designer may have a choice of supplier, and can therefore request information on the ingredients used in the dye, and on the pollution controls used in processing. Some substances are more hazardous than others: the metallic dyes used for navy, black and other dark colours are most likely to accumulate in the ground and leach into groundwater supplies.

## Industrial production or craft?

Produced on an industrial scale, all textiles have pollutant effects. However, when produced on a small scale, environment impact is more controllable, and some environmentally sensitive solutions become practicable. The use of natural plant-based dyes currently makes more sense as part of a small-scale, craft approach, where subtle differences between items enhance their individuality and appeal. Wool, if produced by small

flocks of well cared for sheep, can retain its natural oils, which provide a degree of water-resistance and insulation.

The craft-based approach, while not likely to supply a major proportion of the world's demand, could play an important role in providing ideas about ingredients and processes that might then be adapted for larger-scale operations. For small quantities, craft production can be both more original and more economic, and there should be more opportunity to monitor environment performance.

Craft-scale textile production is widespread in small rural communities in Third World countries. Usually, traditional methods are used, with production predominantly hand-powered. Buying directly from workshops and cooperatives can help support local economies. However, production on an industrial scale in the Third World can be highly polluting, with little regulatory control. Higher prices and fairer world trade agreements might allow some improvement - but only if it is demanded by customers.

## Use and disposal

Textiles usually have to be cleaned during the course of their life - in the case of clothes, perhaps hundreds of times. Dry cleaning currently uses chlorinated solvents such as perchlorethylene, an ozone depleter, and is a very energy-intensive process; fabrics which can only be dry-cleaned should therefore be avoided if possible.

Washing and drying, however, uses considerable energy and water. Man-made fabrics can claim to be energy-saving when they require low-temperature washing, and can be drip-dried. However, these savings have to be set against the energy consumed during their manufacture.

Textiles can be re-used or recycled, to prolong their useful life. Passing on unwanted clothing, carpets and household textiles to other people is obviously the first step. Designers can play a role, perhaps, in removing the social stigma of "second hand" by promoting the use of old or recyled materials.

Good-quality used cotton is often shredded to give a filling for furniture. Wool, a valuable material even when recycled, is used to produce felt, mattress stuffing and even suiting cloth. Plain coloured synthetics can be broken down into fibres and woven into new garments. Multicoloured materials can be compacted and used as padding. A much higher quantity of all fabrics could be recycled, reducing the volume of new materials required.

▲ A traditionally made rag rug, "Jeksen", marketed in large quantities by the Swedish-based furniture retailers Ikea. Traditionally, such rugs were made to recycle household rags, but they can equally well be made from manufacturers' offcuts.

Eventually, if they cannot be indefinitely recycled, materials are disposed of by incineration or landfill. Synthetics can produce significant amounts of energy, but can give off toxic gases. In landfill sites, biodegradability becomes an issue. Pure natural fibres can be composted, and the decomposition of organic material contributes to the methane gas given off by landfill sites, which can be harnessed as energy.

### The design decision

Textile designers should bear in mind the durability and ease of care of the materials they produce. Consideration of the physical construction of the wool or yarn is important, as this can determine how long the fabric can retain its appearance and properties. Care instructions should consider energy use; for example, most moderately dirty cottons are washed at 95 degrees Celsius where 60 degrees would be sufficient.

Designers could consider new uses for recycled fabric. The challenge lies in the development of new types of cloth that use this raw material. Can these be aesthetically attractive as well as being functional? Manufacturers must also consider what happens to waste product during the course of the production process. Can more waste be collected and re-used, as in the paper industry?

## Fashion

Is there a conflict of interest? The fashion industry appears to thrive on waste and excess, with little correlation between wants and needs, and short product life cycles used to maintain consumption. The comfort and pleasure of the user in wearing clothes often appear to be neglected in favour of novelty and creating the right "look", with the result that too many clothes are not particularly human-friendly, let alone environment-friendly. With fashions changing so rapidly, designing long-lasting clothes might appear irrelevant - we should be aiming for flexibility and adaptability, so that clothes can be transformed to meet new themes. Reversible clothing could be one way of achieving flexibility. Another approach is to design "classic" well-made clothes that will continue to appear stylish whatever the passing fashion may be. Many people have already decided to dress this way for economy as well as simplicity.

We also have to consider whether clothes always have to look brand new to be stylish. Many fabrics continue to look attractive when they have aged - even when they have been mended or altered. The attraction for the old and "interesting" is clearly seen in our fondness for antique rugs or curtains. Perhaps designers should consider how their products will age, and aim for materials which do not lose their colour and shape after the first wash.

### Second-hand clothes

The continual throwing-out of wardrobes does provide a form of recycling, although most people are very reluctant to discard clothes, even when there is no realistic prospect of their being worn. Second-hand clothes can be of high fashion interest - as seen by the desire for worn jeans - but in general there is still a reluctance to accept them as a logical part of the normal wardrobe. Some fashion designers are beginning to consider recycled clothes as interesting materials, but so far there has been little serious attempt to design for recycled clothes.

### Fur and leather

Demand for furs is falling as a result of successful campaigning by environmental and animal welfare groups, bringing to the public's attention the suffering endured by farmed as well as trapped animals. Some designers have moved from using real fur to fake fur. Some fake furs are obviously not intended to be realistic, but others aim to be indistinguishable from the real thing - an approach which will surely perpetuate the idea that furs are a suitable clothing material. Fake furs are produced from synthetic or regenerated fibres, with the environment issues mentioned above.

Designers can look for alternatives to leather products from both endangered and non-endangered species. A good example of this is fish leather, a by-product from food production which is an alternative to snakeskin.

### Fashion trends

The fashion industry is predicting that "green" interests will be a strong influence on fashion themes during the 1990s: "eco-fashion", based on the colours of sea, sky and earth, with nature prints and shell jewellery, has been proposed. One of the first collections for the "pure" Nineties, however, from Rifat Ozbek, featured an array of pure white clothes that were not only bleached, but required continual cleaning. It is not yet clear whether the fashion world will simply look upon the environment as another superficial styling gimmick, or whether there will be a real attempt to tackle some of the issues

➤ "Peau de Mer" leather, made from the skins of fish caught for food, which would otherwise go to waste. The process was developed in Australia by Keith Taylor, and the products are marketed in North America where designers are looking for an ecologically acceptable alternative to leather from the skins of exotic animals. Cod, catfish and wolf fish - all caught in the North Atlantic - are used, with care being taken that the methods used do not contribute to over-fishing. The skin is removed when the fish are filleted, and tanned to make it soft and workable. Different species have different markings and textures: catfish is soft and suede-like, while cod is sleek and glazed, resembling lizardskin. Durable and colourfast, the leather cuts well and sews easily.

relating to the resource consumption and pollution created by textile manufacture and use. As in other areas of environmental product design, however, appearance not backed up by reality will cause confusion and attract criticism. The "natural look", which aims to convince consumers that it is environmentally conscious but where none of the major issues relating to the production process have been considered, will have only a short-term appeal as consumer knowledge increases.

Overt "ethnic" looks, a recurring fashion theme, now appear more popular than ever. Katherine Hammet remarks: "Ethnic, ethnic everywhere. It's a rejection of Western values and the ugliness that surrounds us. People are bored with looking rich in Chanel, and want to be interesting and socially responsible."

# *case study* *Junichi Arai fabrics, Japan*

The traditional jacquard weave incorporates the design into the weave, instead of later printing on a pattern. The Nuno Corporation in Tokyo use this technique extensively with undyed, unbleached materials to produce environmentally considered, innovative fabrics. These fabrics, all designed by Junichi Arai, are intended for mass production, and have distinctive features which make them appropriate for clothing or furniture.

"Korean Carrot" is made of undyed wool, using the jacquard technique of three-dimensional textures created by the felted finishing process. The "Basket Weave Pockets" design is a combination of unbleached and undyed fine cotton yarn and knitted tapes which give it an unusual and interesting texture: the pockets in the fabric are raised by using a double weave technique.

Acetate and rayon are mixed in "Zig Zag" to create a puckered texture. The acetate yarn shrinks during the finishing process, and this shrinking, combined with the tight twist of the yarn, produces the mesh pattern and the puckered effect. Again, no dyes are used.

➤ Puckered mesh "Zig Zag".

➤ "Basket Weave Pockets".

▼ "Korean Carrot".

# *case study*    *Novotex "green cotton", Denmark*

◄ ▲ A wide range of colours and textural effects can be achieved with Novotex "green cotton". The fabric is woven to have bounce and spring, and therefore does not require chemical treatment to give it body or to ensure it retains its shape and springiness.

Novotex have produced a cotton fabric which combines an environment-conscious manufacturing process with special shape-retention properties. The fabric is specially designed to minimise the need to use chemical additives, and throughout the dyeing and finishing process pollution is minimised by the use of the most sophisticated purification and monitoring systems.

The cotton fibre is hand-picked in South America; the use of chemical sprays is minimal, as hand-picking means that the cotton can be carefully selected. The company has invested in an organic cotton field, but this does not yet yield enough to offer a commercially viable alternative.

Normally, knitted cotton fabrics are treated with chemicals such as formaldehyde to stabilise them, to ensure that they do not shrink and crease; this can cause allergic reactions in some people if the fabric is worn next to the skin. Novotex cotton is produced by purely mechanical treatments. The yarn is twisted, to give the fabric extra springiness and substance, then the fabric is pre-shrunk, to avoid the need to treat it with chemicals. The qualities of shape and size retention remain even after excessive washing and tumble-drying. The fabric is bleached using hydrogen peroxide, rather than the potentially hazardous chlorine.

The dyeing process frequently causes environmental damage in textile production. Novotex have developed their product in close collaboration with a high technology dyeworks. The fabric is dyed in closed jet systems which minimise water consumption and prevent air pollution. Waste water is purified very thoroughly, with no residue allowed to escape into the watercourses. Natural dyes are used wherever possible. The fabric is used in a wide range of clothing, and has met with consumer approval because of its unusually silky texture, excellent washing properties and durability.

In an attempt to keep improving the environment performance of the product and process, Novotex estimate the environment impact of the different stages in the production of the material, rating current performance as a percentage of the ideal, truly "green", 100 per cent - which of course will never be reached. However, the pursuit of this theoretical objective constantly stimulates further product improvements.

➤ The Novotex plant has been carefully designed to maximise worker safety and comfort.

# *case study*    *Courtaulds Tencel, UK*

Tencel is a new regenerated fibre developed by Courtaulds, designed to be virtually free of the chemical additives which are widely used with cellulose fibres. The production process has also been designed to produce no significant waste products. Conventional viscose rayon is produced using chemicals which can be harmful to the environment if they are contained in effluent, as well as being potentially unpleasant for those involved in the production process. The resulting fibre can also contain small traces of chemicals which may limit its application.

Tencel is produced by dissolving wood pulp in amine oxide, a chemical from the family commonly used in the manufacture of shampoo. The mixture is passed through a continuous dissolving unit to produce a clear but viscous solution, which is filtered and spun into a dilute solution of amine oxide, which precipitates out

➤ **Tencel offers a durable but attractive material suitable for high-fashion clothes.**

the cellulose in filament form. The dilute amine oxide is purified and reconcentrated to remove the water, and then fed back into the process.

The fibre produced is considerably stronger than cotton, polyester or viscose, and is easy to dye and to print. 100 per cent Tencel fibres printed with reactive dyes or pigment require no caustic treatment, thus cutting out a potentially polluting process. Tencel is suitable for woven clothes, home furnishings and speciality non-woven fabrics. Courtaulds intend to use it to extend the applications to which cellulose fibres can be put.

▼ Tencel is easy to dye and print, to achieve a luxurious effect with strong patterns and bright colours.

# *case study* *The Natural Dye Company knitwear, UK*

▼ A selection of jerseys, demonstrating the richness and subtlety of colour which can be achieved using natural dyes.

➤ Bales of wool are hung up to dry after dyeing.

Natural dyes are frequently discussed as an alternative to synthetic dyes. But the large quantities of natural materials that would be required to supply the needs of industrial users mean that natural dyes are unlikely to be a realistic replacement for synthetic dyes; however, they are entirely appropriate for use in relatively small-scale craft industries.

Sarah Burnett, a British knitwear designer, produces elaborate multi-coloured garments with the use of natural dyes. Using tropical fruits, plants and nuts, she has created a wide range of colours. Indigenous materials she gathers herself provide subtle greens, yellows and browns, while the brighter colours are imported from South America, India and Mexico.

The yarns - such as wool, silk and chenille - are dyed in converted farm buildings. Each hand of yarn is washed to make the dye fast, and exact quantities are used to ensure that no dye is wasted.

Natural dyes can be subject to fading in the light. By combining two or more colours in each knit, any fading is subtle, and the overall result continues to be attractive and harmonious.

Although traditional techniques are used to produce the knits, the patterns can be sophisticated, often inspired by the surrounding countryside. Garments have a rather theatrical quality, and are unique pieces, owing to the nature of the dying process which ensures that no two pieces are ever exactly the same.

# *case study*  *Reactivart clothing, UK*

➤ Richard Royal used old sample books from fabric merchants to produce a range of twelve individual jackets.

◄ Sommoli made this outfit from old saris and broken Indian jewellery, for a rich, ethnic effect.

Reactivart is an organisation formed in the UK to promote the use of recycled products in the arts and fashion. Second-hand clothing is re-worked into garments intended for the young, fashion-oriented market. The clothes are intended to be as bright, fun and "trendy" as the clothes from high street fashion outlets, but without any imposed fashion obsolescence.

The organisation wishes to promote clothing recycling on a wider scale, and to encourage the sale of clothes made from recycled fabrics in mass market stores.

▼ Coat designed by Janet Swift, made from old wool jumpers that have been cut up and interlocked into a simple, bright and fun garment.

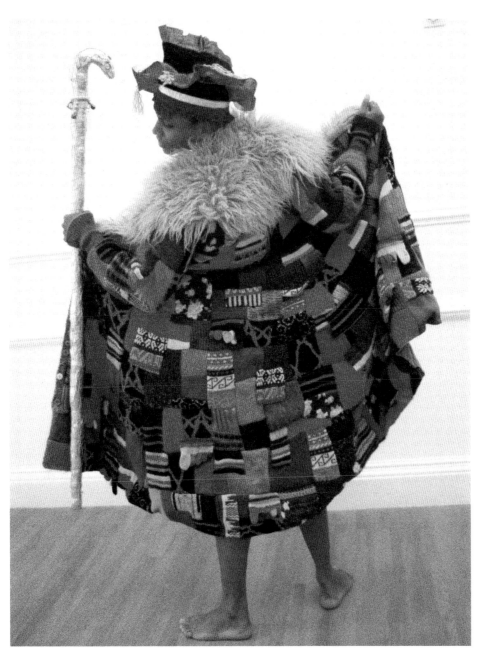

▲ Anne McTavish employed fabric scraps from fashion houses for her hats, which have adaptable shapes formed from wire.

# 8     The changing face of design

If we are to minimise the extent of environment problems design will have to change, because users and consumers of design - individuals and industry - will have to change. Legislation, changing customer priorities and industrial competition will make the pressure for change inevitable, irrespective of designers' personal concerns. The changes that will be necessary will not be minor adjustments or a thin veneer; the inclusion of environment criteria as an integral part of the design process will be one of the most important and far-reaching developments in the history of design. This will create new themes for design, as well as offering the designer a new, more central role.

The designer's task will become more difficult and more important than ever, demanding changes in attitude, education, approach and sophistication. The design skills required may change too, as many economies continue to shift from manufacturing to service-based industries.

## The changing design process

Designers already have to consider a wide range of criteria as part of the design process: marketing, production, financial and technical considerations have to be included. Compared with these, environment considerations could be even more complex and hard to handle. There are very often no clear answers; information is hard to find; guidelines may not be available; so much original research and thinking may be necessary. What general changes might one expect to see in the design process, given the need to incorporate this new criterion?

### Think environment up front

Increasingly, businesses and institutions are assessing their environment performance comprehensively, through tools such as environmental auditing, recognising that good environment performance does not come simply from attempting to improve in one or two areas. The development of a product which is environmentally safer in use or disposal may well be desirable, but if its production consumes

four times as much energy, the net result may be less beneficial.

Designers, equipped with a broad knowledge of environment issues and implications, should be aware of the context within which they are working, and understand the environment performance of the organisation with which they are working. A review of environmental auditing or assessment data may become an essential part of the background briefing of the designer, just as knowledge of the company's marketing strategy, or the institution's philosophy and objectives, are today.

### Ask the right questions

The designer cannot rely on others being well informed. There are, of course, increasing numbers of experts on environment issues, and on the technical issues surrounding them and their possible solutions. It is still the exception, however, for those likely to be commissioning design work to be very knowledgeable themselves on the issues which might appropriately be considered.

The designer must therefore expect to take considerable responsibility for asking the right questions, and raising the relevant issues. By demonstrating an awareness of potential problems, the designer is helping minimise risks to the success of the programme. The unfortunate discovery half-way through a programme of a major problem with the proposed raw

material or production method can be avoided by a thorough consideration, before the start, of all the issues.

### Seek information
It is still difficult to be aware of all the possible environment issues which surround design decisions. In order to keep pace with rapid developments in scientific understanding and the discovery of new causes for concern, the designer must stay in touch with the environmental agenda, by following media coverage, subscribing to environment organisations or demanding regular briefings from professional or trade associations. It is more difficult still to find detailed information on the environment performance of alternative mate-

rials or processes, or to identify sources of supply which are guaranteed to be environment-conscious.

Designers cannot be expected to have the time or specialist knowledge to be able to gather all the information they will need and, indeed, some information may take several years of research to emerge. Some designers may wish to spend an increasing proportion of their time devoted to background information collection and checking details; others will resist spending too much time away from the creative process. Designers can be instigators and commissioners of research, and can ensure that research is built in to the design process. There are already a number of environmental researchers working closely with

▲ ➤ Les Garennes, a housing development in St Quentin en Yvelines near Versailles, France, was used as a one of the EC's Project Monitor case studies (for more details, see page 40). It illustrates that energy-saving design can be used effectively in domestic apartment blocks. Completed in 1985, it comprises 148 apartments in six blocks. Full-height "sunspaces" supply solar-heated air to the living rooms, thermostatically controlled by a fan. Roof-mounted active solar panels heat the water supply. All the windows are double-glazed for insulation. The buildings' dramatic appearance from the south side is due to the large glass and metal sunspaces, which provide extra living space as well as solar power. The average contribution of solar power to the heating requirements was 33 per cent, with a maximum of 41 per cent. Yet the solar design accounted for only 12 per cent of the total building cost. It is anticipated that it will have paid for itself in only twelve years.

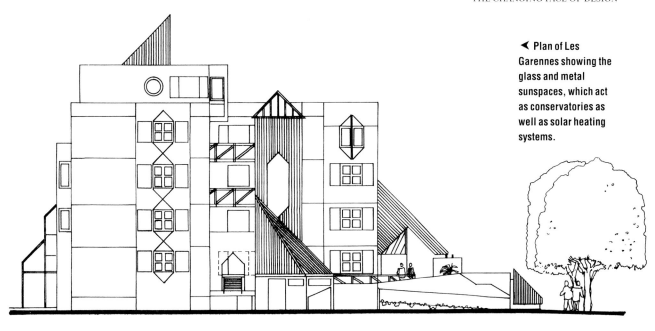

◄ Plan of Les Garennes showing the glass and metal sunspaces, which act as conservatories as well as solar heating systems.

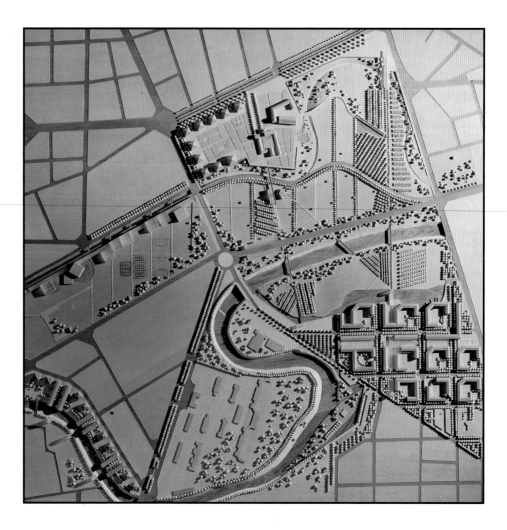

▲ The 1990 Annual Report for the Emess Lighting
Company, designed by David Davies Associates,
makes a contrast to the multi-colour, high-gloss,
extravagant annual reports common in the Eighties.
It adopts a modest and understated style,
communicating honesty and simplicity.

designers, advising them on material specification, or reviewing work at concept
stage to identify any potential problems.
This may become a common working
arrangement. Environment specialists -
who might even be designers who have
chosen to focus on this area - could
become an important part of the core
design team.

**Practical concept development**

The separation of concept and execution
will become increasingly difficult when
environment considerations have to be at
the forefront. Many environment issues
will relate to aspects of execution - the
materials used, the production process
used, how a product will be disposed of,
for example. These questions have to be
addressed during the development of the
design concept itself, not introduced as an
afterthought once the basic concept has
been agreed.

**Closer liaison**

Designers have never been able to work in
isolation; they are necessarily team workers, if sometimes reluctantly. The need to
consider environment issues and executional details at an early stage in the design

◄ ► Model (left) and site plan showing "La Città - Rifugio della Natura", a project designed for the Italian city of Turin by Barcelona architects Martorell, Bohigas, Mackay and Puigdomenech. The aim is to preserve traditional patterns of the countryside - but to do this within the city, by reclaiming land which is no longer needed for industrial purposes. The land would then return to its pre-industrial state, highlighting the lost structures of the traditional countryside before it was built on. One function of the modern city is to preserve history and culture, so it is a logical extension for it to preserve a piece of agricultural history.

process will mean that close partnerships with other contributors to the programme - engineers, printers, construction companies, technologists - will be essential. The designer must establish a capability that goes far beyond styling or pure visual appearance, and should not abdicate responsibility in technical areas. On environment issues - as on other issues such as cost and timing - the designer must be in a position to assess and judge the recommendations and output of a wide range of technical specialists. The fear that concentration on executional constraints inhibits creativity will have to be overcome.

**Assessing the risk of failure**

Environment problems, or risks to health and safety, are often hard to foresee. It will, however, become an increasingly important aspect of the designer's work to minimise the risks arising from the failure of a product or process.

Much of the focus in this area will be on the design of industrial facilities or building developments, where environment impact assessments must anticipate the consequences of modifications to the original design, or of human negligence. The eventual environment impact of a major construction, such as an industrial processing plant or a holiday village development, must be carefully assessed at the planning stage, to minimise the risk of long-term damage to the local ecology. Sophisticated electronic sensing devices may increasingly be used to detect the presence of undesirable gases, or of fire. Once again, the responsibility of the designer stretches further.

These are just some of the ways in which the design process may change to accommodate the new criterion of environment performance. Clearly, each design discipline will evolve differently, but in general terms we should see a broader interpretation of the design process, encompassing the cradle-to-grave aspects of the design and therefore necessarily covering many technical and executional aspects. Information gathering and interpretation will become even more important, and what the designer cannot cover may be sought from a new breed of specialist environment researchers.

## Technology - friend or foe?

There are many fears that rapid technological development has brought with it

➤ Extending the use of garments by designing for reversibility is a theme explored in this cotton jacquard material by Junichi Arai called "Magic Marker", from the Nuno Corporation in Japan. The four-layer weave structure allows a different pattern on each side of the cloth.

increasing environment problems. On the other hand, newer technologies often tend to be less polluting and dangerous than what they replace. While any new development obviously brings with it unknown problems - CFCs were embraced as a major advance when first introduced - there do seem to be many opportunities for using sophisticated technology to improve environment performance. Information technology could, if used properly, eliminate a significant amount of paper use; fibre optics offer an opportunity to save precious metal reserves; microelectronics make possible the miniaturisation of pieces of equipment, leading to possible resource savings, although to increased difficulties in recycling. The intelligent use of new technology should make it possible to derive more value from fewer resources: the use of computer-aided design and manufacture can reduce materials wastage in textiles and other areas; computer-based energy management and fuel control systems will become common in buildings and cars.

Designers may find themselves in the forefront of identifying problems which must be addressed by technology. Sometimes existing technologies may not be able to provide the solution, and the designer may have to stimulate and influence the development of a new technological approach. The role of the designer as the stimulus for, rather than the distant incorporator of, technological advance will again prove challenging and will require interests and skills which may go beyond those areas traditionally regarded as appropriate in design. Just as designers must monitor the environmental agenda carefully, so they must also follow technological developments, to be sure of incorporating the most environmentally advanced technology, or to identify gaps which need to be researched.

Although one underlying theme of environmentalism is a return to a simpler lifestyle and the avoidance of spurious complexity, there is a case for increasing the intelligence of products or buildings as part of increasing efficiency. Energy efficiency is an obvious case, as is failure detection, but increased flexibility for multi-purpose use could also be achieved through greater intelligence.

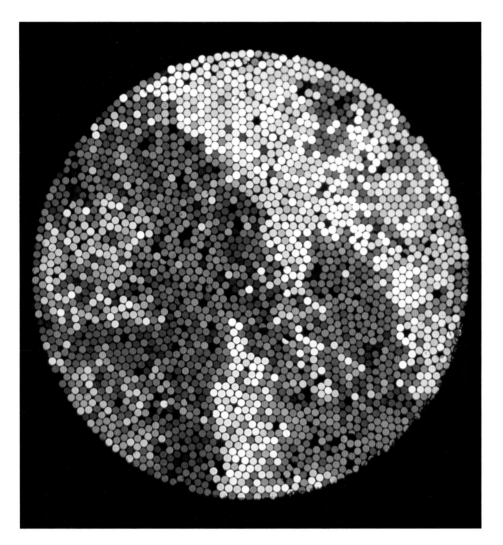

◀ A cross-section of a Thornton Packard glass fibre optic cable, magnified six times, showing the illuminated tips of individual strands. Optical fibres could replace copper cable in telecommunications, thus saving resources, while offering a huge expansion of facilities, such as video-phones, home banking and entertainment.

## Information design and communication

End users' demand for information about products and behaviour will increase steadily as people begin to make choices on the basis of more complex criteria. Information about the environment impact of a product - which may have to encompass ingredients, manufacturing method, use and disposal instructions - will be included on packaging, or in accompanying leaflets. But in most product categories, the information must be presented in a way which is easy and quick to assimilate, and incapable of misinterpretation. Consumers wish to obtain an immediate impression of the environment characteristics of their intended purchase; they also require usage instructions and disposal instructions which make the right behaviour appear simple and desirable.

The development of information systems which are at once comprehensive, easy to absorb and motivating will give major scope for graphic design. The growth of products which are sold in many different countries will pose the challenge of how complex information can be communicated by the use of visual symbols.

Official eco-labelling systems will be one aspect of information provision, but these will not cover all categories, and will necessarily be a summarised version of more detailed information which may well have to be communicated in some other form elsewhere.

Information about the product or service will become a part of the product offer that is valued in its own right. It therefore may assume a much higher profile than in the past, when ingredients, technical specifications or usage instructions were consigned to tiny print on the back or base of the package or brochure. This may suggest, in some categories, less reliance on borrowed interest to give the product appeal, and more use of design themes which stem directly from the product itself.

Opportunities for information design may well expand far beyond the obvious area of product information provision. In many countries, government campaigns to encourage changes in public behaviour will be launched, perhaps in areas such as energy conservation and recycling. These will require co-ordinated communications

▲ General Motors'
"Sunraycer" car,
competing in the 1987
Pentax World Solar
Challenge, the first
international race for
solar-powered cars,
run between Darwin
and Adelaide,
Australia. It was the
winner, taking five and
a half days to travel the
1,950 miles, at an
average speed of 41.6
mph. It is powered by
7,200 photovoltaic
cells, joined to form a
hood over the top and
back of the vehicle.

▼ The "Little Beaver"
chair and stool,
manufactured by Vitra
International in
Switzerland, is
constructed out of
packaging cardboard.
Designer Frank O.
Gehry believes that
everyday items which
are usually discarded
can be recycled into
serviceable objects.

▲ In this solar power station in the Mojave Desert in California, run by the Edison Electric Company, computer-controlled mirrors on the desert surface track the sun and reflect its radiation on to a 20-storey reflector tower. This concentrates the heat on to tubes containing synthetic oil which reaches a very high temperature. The heat is used to produce steam, which drives the turbines that generate the electricity.

programmes, supported by practical aspects of infrastructure development.

Growth in public transport systems will demand not only new ideas in vehicles and route development, but also excellent signage systems, new ways of delivering up-to-the-minute information to passengers, and the creation of station surroundings which are aesthetic and practical.

Increasing use of computers, and of computer-dependent services such as financial services, will create a demand for designers who can improve the user-friendliness of both hardware and software. The design of on-screen information can be significantly improved by the application of principles based on an understanding of how people react to visual stimuli. "Intelligent" products, and new services based on information provision, will meet with wide success only if information can be provided in a highly accessible, sympathetic and attractive way.

## Future design themes and styles

The inclusion of environment criteria will inevitably influence design styles. New themes will emerge, stimulated partly by changes in tastes, partly by legislation and partly by a need to incorporate new practical considerations. Many designers will look upon this development as an oppor-

tunity to introduce new thoughts and sources of inspiration, not necessarily driven by evangelical fervour, but rather by a desire to be in the vanguard of innovative and distinctive design.

Themes beginning to emerge in consumer markets in Northern Europe and North America include a new focus on quality and value, and the rejection of purely quantitative consumption goals; a desire for products or buildings designed to last, rather than created with built-in obsolescence; an interest in the ideas surrounding a product, in addition to the product itself, and the promotion of "anti-consumerism" as a marketing platform. Selling products on the basis of encouraging customers to buy them only if they really need them may currently seem like a marketing disaster, but one clothing company, Esprit in the USA, is already adopting this approach - and is encouraging customers to pass the clothes on to someone else once they have finished with them. "Less is more" could become a potent and distinguishing message.

Inevitably, if "eco-themes" become popular there will be attempts to use them purely as styling themes irrespective of the real performance of the product. Spurious green labels initially undermined "green product" marketing activities, and the bandwagoning of green design themes for products which are not in fact truly

◄ ▲ The German retailers Tengelmann, wanting to improve the image of their own-brand chocolates, focused on the plastic tray - could it be replaced with a more natural alternative? In partnership with the wafer manufacturer Loser, a wafer tray was developed that tasted good. It does not taint the chocolates, and contains any leakage should they break. This idea could be used for the millions of plastic trays used in chocolate boxes every year.

environment-conscious must be resisted. Environment-conscious design must not be seen as a styling exercise - indeed, it is not truly related to style at all. However, some obvious new styles may well emerge, based on a desire to embody in the look of a product the high importance given to environment considerations during its design and development.

● Natural, crafts heritage, sustainable: the use of natural materials, in an "untreated" form, particularly in the production of furniture, building materials and textiles.

● Utility, efficiency: the obvious use of recycled materials, emphasising sustainability, with a design style based on the requirements of function.

● Minimalist: style emphasising economy in the use of materials; an absence of non-functional, purely decorative features; dramatic shapes to create interest and impact, or a return to classic simplicity.

● Multi-purpose adaptability: flexible design which can be changed to add interest, avoiding the need for replacement out of boredom; which can be updated, renovated or re-presented, with minimal additional use of materials, to prolong life; which uses "added intelligence", or dismantleable components.

Themes of nostalgia for a pre-industrial world may sit alongside deliberate use of "hi-tech" associations. Science may serve as a stimulus just as much as nature will, with the increasing acceptance of the need for advanced technology to play a role in solving problems, together with a simpler, more sustainable lifestyle.

What themes may become less commonly used in design? It seems certain

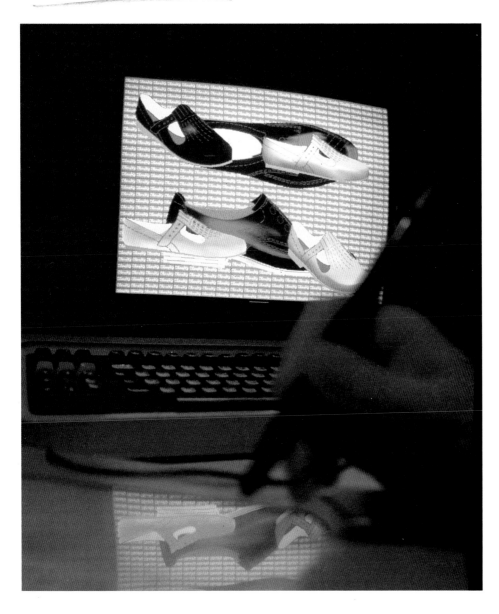

◄ A designer at the UK shoe manufacturers, Clarke, uses a light pen to work on computer-aided design and manufacturing techniques, which improve the speed and efficiency of the design process. High precision and a detailed information base ensure exact sizes for maximum user comfort. The designer can view the three-dimensional images on screen, eliminating the need for prototypes and materials wastage.

➤ A drawing made by a pupil at St Kilian's Deutsche Schule in Clonksea, Dublin, Eire, as part of a schools project run by The Body Shop. Children were taught to create new materials by weaving into sheets of paper items related to their environment. This painting of a bird in its nest uses leaves to add dimension and atmosphere to the basic paper which was made from lokta from Nepal (see pages 130-33). About 150 schools took part in the project, which is due to be repeated in the UK and in Hong Kong.

▼ Graphics to accompany a series of television programmes on environmental issues for children, designed by Gary Rowland Associates and printed on recycled paper. Children demonstrate a high level of environmental concern, and are keen to learn more. Much of the educational and promotional material produced for them demonstrates that it is possible to be environment-conscious without being dull or unattractive.

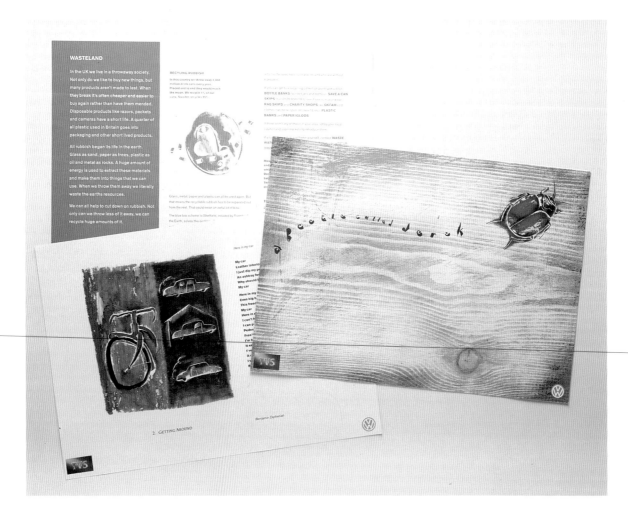

that the excessive use of resource-consuming decoration, which does not enhance functionality, will become unpopular in many countries, although the importance of elaborate measures to enhance appearance in Japan may prove a countervailing pressure here.

Design which has an "inhuman" face, because it is remote, unintelligible, or difficult to access or use, will be at odds with environment-conscious design. Design must now aim to involve users, inform them, educate them and, often, introduce them to technology. Design must not place products on a pedestal and make them impenetrable; on the contrary, it must be highly sympathetic to user needs. A major challenge will be that of producing minimalist design which is warm and friendly, rather than cold, over-sophisticated and obscure. Design which focuses solely on function, to the exclusion of any aesthetic satisfaction of the user, does not contribute as much as it could to the enhancement of the quality of life.

## The social context of design

Environment is not simply a practical issue; it is also a moral one. The idea that, as part of their professional code of practice, designers should aim to minimise the environment impact of their work has been accepted in several institutions. Just as the medical profession observes the Hippocratic Oath, so designers have been urged to take responsibility for a "green ethic", because of the central role they play in influencing the environment performance of so many things.

Very many other moral issues are now emerging as possible influences on public purchasing and behaviour. The welfare of animals, fair trade with Third World countries, the treatment of minorities, military expenditure and many other issues are rapidly becoming part of the marketing agenda, as campaigning groups provide consumers with more information about the activities of companies and governments, and as companies begin to use very broad aspects of their corporate behaviour to establish a desirable image and achieve further differentiation in the market place.

It is beyond the scope of this book to begin to examine the role of the designer in addressing this wider sphere of ethical and social issues. But it is not unrealistic to expect that, irrespective of the designer's own moral code, ethical issues will become additional criteria in the design process, through the mechanism of consumer preference. Once again, the central, influential position of the designer provides a real opportunity to effect change.

The ability of designers to identify and solve problems through insight, and their mastery of a wide range of valuable skills, equip them to make a significant contribution across a very wide area. Designers have always striven for a better way of doing things - now that better way can embrace environmental, ethical and social issues, too. Vast efforts have been

▲ Children's play structures designed by Eiji Hiyama of Papyrus, Tokyo, and made from cardboard. Simple houses and towers are joined together with elastic bands; stored flat, they can easily be erected by the children themselves.

expended in addressing problems which were not real problems - how to create a more chic or tasteful consumer durable, for example. The diversion of design skills into the many areas where real problems wait to be solved would provide challenging new outlets: appropriate housing and products for Third World countries, products for the handicapped or elderly, pollution-abatement equipment. These are types of design work that have been the "Cinderella" areas, unlikely to grab the glittering prizes or build reputations in the way that the styling of a new motorcycle can. Perhaps this will now change, as social responsibility becomes a market-driven, user-driven benefit, in addition to a matter of personal feelings. Designing for the common good may come to be seen as a commercial necessity rather than an ideal.

Designers have often aspired to radicalism; many times that radicalism has been solely related to aesthetics, or has not created a net improvement in the utility or social impact of the item designed. Radical design now has new outlets, as many solutions to environment and social problems will be unexpected and unconventional. Only by re-thinking some basic assumptions about function, tastes and lifestyle will we be able to move any significant way towards a more sustainable way of living.

## Training and education for design

Many design courses continue virtually to ignore environment issues, thus equipping students poorly even for current demands. There can be little doubt that it is essential to include information about environment issues and their relationship to the design process in the core curriculum. Equally important is the development of an understanding that environment is not a separate, specialist subject which designers can choose to be interested in or not, but rather one basic criterion against which all design work should be assessed.

The relative newness of the subject means that good teaching material is only just emerging, and there is a lack of good case histories to form the basis of projects. This may mean that students will have a real opportunity to conduct original research, and to produce material which may be of practical use beyond its value to them as a learning experience. Students may well be relatively better informed about environment issues generally than their teachers, and thus the two parties can work constructively together to apply their knowledge of design disciplines to environment problems.

In the longer term, we may wish to question design training programmes which are highly specialised. The design generalist may have a resurgence, because of the importance of being able to understand not just the entire design process, but also to see how it fits into a broader context. The re-designing of our society to minimise environmental problems will demand an integrated approach - one which recognises the impact that one thing has on another. Breadth of experience and vision will be valued, as we attempt to cope with large-scale, apparently impenetrable and highly complex problems.

In order to anticipate problems and devise inspired solutions, designers must be equipped with an understanding of subjects which stretch far beyond the boundaries of traditional design teaching. Life sciences, behavioural sciences, ecology, anthropology and many other areas may come to be seen as a necessary part of the design curriculum, alongside computer programming and marketing. Breadth of formal education may be further supplemented by an increased focus on travel and practical experience, reflecting the importance of learning from different cultures, and the need to master the most practical, executional aspects of design just as much as the generation of ideas.

Designers have an opportunity to exert considerable influence, if they choose to do so. But this influence will have to be supported by knowledge, open-mindedness and flexibility, and an ability to go on learning. The primadonna designer driven by opinions on aesthetics alone will be eclipsed by a more cerebral breed of well-informed, technology-literate but equally creative designer.

Criticism of the superficiality and faddish elitism of design could become a thing of the past. Designers can now prove that they are an essential tool in planning a sustainable future.

▶ The SL48 Solar Lantern, designed for BP Solar International by Moggridge Associates, converts sunlight into electricity using solar cells, providing a 40-watt equivalent light for up to four hours. It is lightweight and portable, designed to operate in remote areas in Africa, and requires virtually no maintenance.

# Further reading

**General**

*Design und Ökologie,*
Bayerisches Staatsministerium für
Wirtschaft und Verkehr, 1990.

John Elkington and Tom Burke,
*The Green Capitalists,*
Gollancz, 1987.

*Environmental Auditing,*
International Chamber of Commerce,
1989.

*Environmental Guidelines for World
Industry,*
International Chamber of Commerce,
1990.

Edward Goldsmith and Nicholas
Hildyard,
*The Earth Report: The Essential Guide to
Global Ecological Issues,*
Mitchell Beazley, second editon 1990.

Waldemar Hopfenbeck,
*Management und Marketing: Konzepte,
Instrumente, Praxis beispiele,*
Verlag Moderne Industrie, 1990.

Norman Myers, ed.,
*The Gaia Atlas of Planet Management,*
Pan, 1985.

*Our Common Future: Report of The World
Commission on Environment and
Development,*
Oxford University Press, 1987.

Victor Papanek,
*Design for The Real World,*
Thames and Hudson, 1985.

Jeremy Rifkin,
*Entropy - Into The Greenhouse World,*
Bantam, 1987.

J.C. Van Weenen,
*Waste Prevention: Theory and Practice,*
Van Weenen, 1990.

David Wann,
*Biologic: Environmental Protection by
Design,*
Johnson Books, 1990.

Georg Winter,
*Business and the Environment,*
McGraw Hill, 1988.

**Architecture and interior design**

Debra Lynn Dadd,
*The Non-Toxic Home,*
Jeremy P. Tarcher, Los Angeles,1986.

*The Good Wood Guide,*
Friends of The Earth, 1990.

David Pearson,
*The Natural House,*
Gaia Books, 1989.

*Project Monitor: a series of case studies
illustrating passive solar architecture in the
European Community,*
Directorate General Xll of the
Commission of the European
Communities, 1987 – .

Robert Sardinsky and Jon Klusmire,
*Resource-Efficient Housing Guide,*
Rocky Mountain Institute, Colorado,
1987-88.

Dr Anton Schneider,
*Working Papers in Building Biology,*
Institute of Building Biology,
Neubeuern, Germany, 1986.

Jarmul Seymour,
*Reducing Energy Consumption in
Buildings,*
Vols Tech Asst, 1988.

Ralph Lee Smith,
*Smart House,*
GP Publishing, Maryland, 1988.

**Product design**

Paul Burrall,
*Green Design,*
The Design Council, 1991.

*Methods to Manage and Control Plastic
Waste,*
US Environmental Protection Agency,
US Department of Commerce,1990.

Vince Packard,
*The Waste Makers,*
Longmans, Green & Co., 1961.

K.J.A. De Waal and W.J. Van den
Brink, eds.,
*Proceedings of the Second European
Conference on Environmental Technology,
Amsterdam,*
Martinus Nijhoff, Dordrecht, 1987.

**Packaging design**

Debra Lynn Dadd,
*The Earthwise Consumer,*
Mill Valley, California, 1989.

John Elkington and Julia Hailes,
*The Green Consumer Guide,*
Gollancz,1988.

*Packaging and Resources,*
Industry Council for Packaging and
the Environment, 1990.

**Print and graphic design**

*The Greenpeace Guide to Paper,*
Greenpeace, Washington, D.C., 1990.

*Guide to Recycled Paper,*
Anderson Fraser Ltd, London, 1991.

*North American Factbook,*
Pulp and Paper Magazine, San
Francisco, 1990.

*Printing Ink Handbook,*
National Association of Printing Ink
Manufacturers, Harrison, New York,
1990.

*Recycled Printing and Writing Paper,*
American Paper Institute, New York,
1990.

*Recycling in The States,*
National Solid Waste Management
Association, Washington, D.C., 1989.

**Textile design**

Robin Anson,
"The Green Fibre Issue",
*Manufacturing Clothier,* volume 70, June
1989.

Dr Ulrich Sewekow,
"Natural Dyes - An Alternative To
Synthetic Dyes",
*Meilliard Textilberichte,* volume 68, 1988.

Trevor Shaw,
"Environmental Issues in the Wool
Textile Industry",
*Proceedings of the Eighth International
Wool Textile Research Conference,
volume 4,*
The International Wool Secretariat
Development Centre, Ilkley, 1990.

# Where to get information

## Belgium

Commission of The European
Communities
(Environment and Consumer
Protection Services)
Rue de la Loi 200
1049 Brussels

European Environmental Bureau
Rue de Luxembourg 20
1040 Brussels

Network for Environmental
Technology Transfer
Square de Meeus 25
Brussels

## France

Agence Nationale pour la
Recupération et l'Elimination des
Déchets
"Les Transformeurs"
2 Square La Fayette
BP 406-49004 Angers

Organisation de Coopération et de
Développement Economique
2 Rue André Pascal
75775 Paris Cedex 16

Programme des Nations Unies pour
l'Environnement (PNUE) - Bureau
Industrie
39-43 Quai André Citroën
75739 Paris Cedex 15

## Germany

Bund für Umwelt und Naturschutz
Deutschland
Im Rheingarten 7
5300 Bonn 3

Bundesminister für Umwelt,
Naturschutz und Reaktorsicherheit
Postfach 12 06 29
Kennedyallee 5
5300 Bonn 1

Institut für Baubiologie und Ökologie
Holzham 25
8201 Neubeuern

Öko-Institut
Binsengrün 34a
7800 Freiburg

Ökotest-Test Magazin
Postfach 11 14 52
6000 Frankfurt 11

Umweltbundesamt
Bismarckplatz 1-3
1000 Berlin 33

## The Netherlands

Greenpeace International
Keizersgracht 176
1016 Amsterdam

## Switzerland

International Environmental Bureau
61 Route de Chene
1208 Geneva

Worldwide Fund for Nature
1196 Gland

## UK

Association for The Conservation of
Energy
9 Sherlock Mews
London W1

Centre for Alternative Technology
Llwyngwen Quarry
Machynlleth
Wales

Centre for Environmental Technology
Imperial College of Science and
Technology
48 Princes Gardens
London SW7 1LU

Chartered Society of Designers
29 Bedford Square
London WC1

Design Council
Haymarket
London W1

Department of Trade & Industry,
Environment Unit
Ashdown House
123 Victoria Street
London SW1E 6RB

DTI Environmental Enquiry Point
Warren Spring Laboratory
Gunnels Wood Road
Stevenage
Hertfordshire SG1 2BX

Ecological Design Association
20 High Street
Stroud
Gloucestershire GL5 1AS

The Environment Council
80 York Way
London N1 9AG

Friends of The Earth International
26-28 Underwood Street
London N1 7JQ

The Industry Committee for
Packaging and The Environment
(INCPEN)
161-166 Fleet Street
London EC4A 2DP

Intermediate Technology
Development Group
Myson House
Railway Terrace
Rugby
Warwickshire

## USA

American Paper Institute
260 Madison Avenue
New York
NY 10016

American Planning Association
1776 Massachusetts Avenue NW
Suite 704
Washington DC 20036

American Recycling Market
PO Box 577
Ogdenssburg
NY 13669

Center for The Study of Responsive
Law
153 P Street NW
Washington DC 20005

Council for Economic Priorities
30 Irving Place
New York
NY 10003

Environmental Action Coalition
625 Broadway
New York
NY 10012

Environmental Defence Fund
257 Park Avenue South
New York
NY 10010

Environmental Protection Agency
Office of Public Affairs
401 M Street SW
Washington DC 20460

Friends of The Earth
218 D Street
Washington DC 20003

Graphic Arts Technical Foundation
4615 Forbes Avenue
Pittsburgh
PA 15213

Inform Inc.
381 Park Avenue South
New York
NY 10016

National Association of Printing Ink
Manufacturers
47 Halstead Avenue
Harrison
NY 10528

National Audubon Society
950 Third Avenue
New York
NY 10022

Rainforest Alliance
270 Lafayette Street
Suite 512
New York
NY 10012

Rocky Mountain Institute
1739 Snowmass Creek Road
Snowmass
Colorado 81654 9199

Sierra Club
330 Pennsylvania Avenue NW
Washington DC 20003

US Consumer Product Safety
Commission
Office of Public Affairs
Washington DC 20207

World Resources Institute
1709 New York Avenue NW
Suite 230
Washington DC 20006

Worldwatch Institute
1776 Massachusetts Avenue NW
Washington DC 20036

# Picture credits

**The author and publishers would like to thank the following for providing the illustrations, or permission to use the illustrations, in this book.**

AEG (UK) Ltd, Slough (pp. 84 top and bottom, 85)

Alberts & Van Huut, Amsterdam (pp. 9, 57, 58 top and bottom)

Mara Amats, London; photo: Shaun Roberts (pp. 131, 132 top, 135, 136 bottom, 137 bottom)

K.K. Arai Creation System, Tokyo (pp. 137 top, 144, 145 top and bottom, 160)

Armstrong Associates, London (p. 44 bottom)

Banks and Miles, London (pp. 128 top and bottom, 129 top, centre and bottom)

Javier Barba, Barcelona; photo: Lluís Casals (pp. 10, 11, 37 top, 39, 66, 67 top and bottom)

Yorrick Benjamin, London (p. 77 top)

Bio Pack, Lippstadt (p. 100)

The Body Shop, Littlehampton, Sussex (pp. 108 top and bottom, 109 top and bottom, 166 top); photo: Shaun Roberts (pp. 132 bottom, 133)

Clare Brass, Silvio Caputo/02, Milan (p. 75 centre)

British Technology Group, London (pp. 102, 103)

Neville Brody and Jon Wozencroft; photo: Shaun Roberts (pp. 126, 127 top and bottom)

Sarah Burnett/The Natural Dye Company, Stanbridge, Dorset (pp. 150, 151)

Busse Design, Ulm (p. 33 top)

Courtaulds Textiles, London (p. 148); photo: Hannah (pp. 138, 139); photo: Shaun Roberts (p. 149)

Cousins Design, New York (p. 22 top)

David Davies Associates Ltd, London (pp. 18, 158 bottom)

Delta Design/Michael Conrad and Dieter Raefler, Stuttgart (p. 79)

Julienne Dolphin-Wilding (pp. 80, 81 top, 80-81)

Duffy Design, Minneapolis (pp. 17, 99 bottom, 117, 122)

ECD Partnership, London (pp. 40, 43, 156 left, 157 top); photo: A. Isola (p. 42); photo: O. Sebart (pp. 156-7)

Environmental Picture Library; photo: Greg Glendell (p. 30 top)

Falkiners Fine Papers Ltd, London; photo: Shaun Roberts (pp. 130 bottom, 131 top, 132 top)

General Motors Corporation, Detroit (pp. 88, 89 top and bottom)

© Greenpeace, London; photo: Menzel (p. 30 bottom); photo: D. Merjenburgh 1989 (p. 13)

Grolsch (UK) Ltd, Andover (p. 33 bottom)

Gruppen for by-og landskabsplan-laegning a/s, Kolding (p. 63)

Habitat Designs Ltd, London (p. 28 left and right)

Thomas Herzog, Munich (p. 64); photo: Schenkirz (p. 65 top and bottom)

Eiji Hiyama/Papyrus, Tokyo (pp. 74, 75 bottom, 167)

Holsting & Engelund I/S, Arhus (p. 62)

ICI Biological Products Division, London (p. 32 top and bottom)

Ikea Ltd, London (p. 141)

Irma A/S, Copenhagen (p. 16)

Jet Pen, Berlin and Paris; photo: Shaun Roberts (p. 70)

Junghans Uhren GmbH, Schramberg (p. 69)

Thierry Kazazian/02, Paris (p. 72)

Khadi Handmade Papers, Chichester (pp. 29 top, centre, bottom, 150 top)

Kreon nv, Antwerp (p. 71 bottom)

Dorian Kurz, Stuttgart (p. 73)

Lammbräu, Neumarkt/König Kommunikations, Nürnberg (p. 20 left)

Lintas: Hamburg GmbH, Hamburg (pp. 20 right, 21 bottom)

Marks & Spencer plc, London (p. 119)

The Geoff Marsh Partnership, Tonbridge (pp. 82, 83)

Martorell, Bohigas and Mackay, Barcelona; photo: CB, Barcelona (pp. 41 top and bottom, 158 top, 159)

Masters Corporation, Connecticut; photo: R. Perron (pp. 60, 61)

McKz Peau de Mer, Cleveland, Ohio (p. 143)

Mobil Oil Corporation (p. 105)

Moggridge Associates, London (p. 169)

Newell & Sorrell, London (pp. 114 centre and bottom, 115, 125)

Leif Nørgaard, Denmark (p. 47)

Frits Nossbaum/02, Copenhagen (p. 155)

Novotex, Ikast (pp. 14, 147); photo: Shaun Roberts (p. 146 top and bottom)

Osram Ltd, Wembley (p. 19 top)

Packaging Innovation, London (pp. 97, 104)

Parachute/Parnass Pelly Ltd, Montreal (p. 44 top)

The Parnham Trust, Beaminster (pp. 45 top and bottom, 76)

The Partners, London (p. 118 top)

Peake, Short and Partners, London (pp. 52, 53 top and bottom, 54 top right and left, bottom, 55 top and bottom)

Gustav Peichl, Vienna (pp. 48, 49)

Pentagram Design, London (p. 71 top)

Michael Peters Ltd, London (pp. 99 top, 107 bottom, 118 bottom)

Private collection; photo: Shaun Roberts (p. 37 bottom)

Procter & Gamble Ltd, Newcastle-upon-Tyne (pp. 31, 107 top, 110 top and bottom, 111)

Ritva Puotila, Tampere, Finland; photo: Domus (p. 136 top)

Reactivart, London (pp. 152 top and bottom, p. 153 top and bottom)

Reed Corrugated Cases, Cowley (pp. 92, 93)

Richard Rogers Partnership, London; photo: Eamonn O'Mahony (p. 51)

Chris Rose/Friends of the Earth, London (p. 27 top)

Gary Rowland Associates, London (pp. 27 bottom, 101, 166)

SAS, Stockholm (p. 46)

Sams Design, London (p. 23)

Science Photo Library; photo: Alex Bartel (pp. 24-5); photo: Martin Dohrn (p. 161); photo: Peter Menzel p. 162 top); photo: Cowell Georgia (p. 163); photo: Jerry Mason/New Scientist (p. 165)

Junko Shimada, Paris; photo: Stéphane Couturier (p. 36)

Paul Smith Ltd, London (p. 50 top and bottom)

SustainAbility Ltd, London (p. 21 top)

TAG, Grenoble (p. 26)

Tengelmann Warenhandelsgesell-schaft, Wiesbaden (pp. 96, 164 top and bottom)

Umweltbundesamt, Berlin (p. 19 bottom)

Varta Ltd, Staines, Middlesex (p. 22 bottom)

Vitra GmbH, Weil am Rhein (p. 162 bottom)

Volvo, Ipswich (pp. 86 top and centre, 87)

Kijuro Yahagi, Tokyo (pp. 91, 124, 125)

Yellow Design, Günter Horntrich (pp. 94, 112 top and bottom, 113)

Zanussi Ltd, Newbury (p. 35)

# Index